CREATIVE QUESTIONS ON CHRISTIAN LIVING

Contemporary Discussion Series

by
Ralph Heynen

CREATIVE QUESTIONS ON CHRISTIAN LIVING

Contemporary Discussion Series

by
Ralph Heynen

BAKER BOOK HOUSE
Grand Rapids, Michigan

ISBN: 0-8010-4038-8

Seventh printing, June 1979

PHOTOLITHOPRINTED BY CUSHING - MALLOY, INC.
ANN ARBOR, MICHIGAN, UNITED STATES OF AMERICA
1979

FOREWORD

In our Christ-centered hospital, one of our chaplains, the Rev. Ralph Heynen, has developed a method by which group dynamics can be applied to the study of the Bible. In discussion classes an attempt is made to make the truths of Scripture relevant to the problems of everyday living. A set of open-ended questions is used to guide and stimulate group discussion in the Christian Living Classes. The success of this method has been evidenced by the lively and active interest shown by the participants.

This emphasis on group discussion has been growing within the church and its various organizations. In many churches a number of small groups meet for sharing and mutual study. This is a wholesome thing, for it provides an effective means of discovering the teachings of the Bible in daily life. In this no one is an expert; each member is able to contribute from his own experience and thus help others to gain insights into the practical application of the teachings of the Bible.

We are pleased that these Studies in Christian Living are now made available to the public. If properly used they can be an excellent aid to make group meetings more meaningful. It is important for all of us to have an opportunity to talk about what our faith in Christ means to us.

The author has twenty-four years of experience in hospital chaplaincy. Out of the rich experience of close contact with many people he has written three books on various phases of Christian mental health.

We heartily commend this booklet to you, fully assured that it will be a means to make your study of the Word a means for spiritual growth and development in the Christian life.

Stuart Bergsma, M.D., Superintendent
Pine Rest Christian Hospital

INTRODUCTION

The aim of this manual is to encourage group discussion on the truth of Scripture as related to some basic questions of Christian living. It calls attention to a number of subjects that the Christian faces in today's world.

These lessons have been selected from the discussion materials prepared for use in the Christian Living classes conducted by the chaplains at Pine Rest Christian Hospital. Since there are a large number of small discussion groups in our churches, these guide questions are presented to stimulate an active interest in practical subjects taken from the Bible.

It is suggested that the group read the Bible passage designated and then move directly into the questions. No introduction need be given by the group leader.

Most of the questions do not allow for a simple "yes" or "no" answer. Nor should the leader allow himself to be caught in a mere question and answer period. The questions must be used to stimulate discussion among the members of the group. It is more important to take up the questions that are of the greatest interest to the group rather than to try to cover each question thoroughly.

Room should also be left for personal initiative. The most successful meetings are those that encourage original thinking, rather than a rehashing of hackneyed ideas and concepts.

This discussion method has been used successfully for a number of years in a variety of groups and by a number of different leaders. It has proved an effective means of obtaining lively group involvement. This should be the aim of every society meeting and Bible class within the church.

This manual is offered in the hope that it may serve as an incentive to make the Bible more relevant to everyday Christian living.

CONTENTS

THE SERMON ON THE MOUNT

NEW TESTAMENT PARABLES

GOSPEL CHARACTERS

CHARACTERS FROM ACTS

THE EPISTLES

1. Cain—Personal Involvement
Genesis 4:1-15

1. If Cain lived today he would be considered a member of the church. He worshiped. What was wrong with his worship? Do you feel this is still found today?

2. Was Cain a bad person, or was he a man who fell into sin? What is the difference?

3. Cain's sin began with envy. Are any of us free from envy? Is this something natural to all men, or do we learn this as children? How can you overcome it?

4. In verses 6 and 7 Cain is warned about his anger. How does God suggest that he conquer it? Do you feel that this is also the way we must overcome hostility and anger?

5. Was Cain really "his brother's keeper"? Was he supposed to be?

6. Today we talk much about "non-involvement." A girl is attacked in a busy neighborhood but no one helps. What is wrong with this attitude? Why is it so common today?

7. Can a person become too involved with the problems of others? Should parents be involved in the problems of their married children?

8. If there is an accident along the highway, is it our duty to stop and help? Some doctors have been sued for the assistance they gave to accident victims; as a result a number of doctors refuse to give aid. What do you think of this?

9. Do you think you should pick up a hitch-hiker?

10. Many countries are vastly overpopulated, while we have considerable surplus and much waste land. Should we liberalize our immigration laws so that more of these people could live in our country?

11. How are we our brother's keeper in a spiritual way?

2. Lot—Making a Foolish Choice
Genesis 13:5-13

1. Lot lived in Abraham's camp for many years. Did he share in Abraham's faith in God?

2. What was Lot's motive when he made his choice to move toward Sodom? Is this kind of choice always sinful in itself?

3. Is it wrong to place ourselves in a position where temptation is found? Can we avoid temptations?

4. Couldn't Lot have moved into Sodom to use his influence to change that godless city? Was it wrong for him to take a position on the city council?

5. Do you think Lot's wife was worse than Lot? Why did she turn into a pillar of salt?

6. Why was Lot and his family so reluctant to leave Sodom when the angel called them?

7. Do you think it was just and fair that God should destroy Sodom and Gomorrah, since there were also many children in those cities?

8. Lot was a man with a divided heart. Part of him loved the world, and part of him served God. Why is it difficult for a person to live this way?

9. How can we overcome the spirit of worldliness that is in us?

10. Do you think there is more worldliness today than there was fifty years ago?

11. In II Peter 2:7 Lot is called "righteous Lot." How can you describe a man like this as "righteous"?

3. Lot's Wife—A Divided Heart

Genesis 19:12-28

Jesus said: "Remember Lot's wife."—Luke 17:32

1. Lot's wife had the privilege of living in the same camp with Abraham. She must have taken part in the sacrifices. Did she also share in his faith?

2. It is said that Lot moved into Sodom, but that his wife allowed Sodom to move into her soul. Is this true? Do you think she was worse than Lot?

3. Do you feel that a woman has more of a tendency than a man has to become attached to earthly things?

4. Why were these people so reluctant to move out of Sodom when the angel called them?

5. Evidently the children of Lot had intermarried with the children of Sodom. What does this show about the family life of Lot? Do you think the daughters of Lot show the influence of Sodom, or was this the influence of parental training?

6. Lot's wife turned to look back. This does not seem to be such a serious offense. Why did the Lord punish her so severely?

7. Lot's wife was a person with a divided heart. Don't you feel that all of us have some of this in our lives? What is wrong with the divided heart?

8. Do you think Lot's wife really turned into a pillar of salt?

9. This account gives us a picture of the real danger of materialism. Why is there so much materialism in the church today? What should the church do about it?

10. Why did Jesus want us to "remember Lot's wife"?

4. Rebekah—A Scheming Mother
Genesis 27:5-29

1. The marriage between Isaac and Rebekah was arranged by Abraham's servant. Is this a good way to arrange a marriage? How much control should parents exercise in the choice of a mate?

2. What is wrong in a family when the mother favors one son and the father another? Does this explain the difference between Esau and Jacob?

3. Isaac was known to have a rather weak character. Do you think it was better that Rebekah took the lead in the family? Should the father be the head of the house?

4. It is commonly stated that mothers are taking a more prominent role in the family and that fathers are taking a lesser role. Is this true? Do you think this is good?

5. Rebekah thought Isaac was making a mistake when he was going to bless Esau. Don't you think it was her duty to use some means to prevent this, since God had told her that Jacob was to have the blessing? Should we not make use of means?

6. Is it ever right to use deception to gain a good purpose? We sometimes use a form of deception to get our children to do what we feel is good for them; is this always bad?

7. What is the difference between being clever and being deceptive?

8. What was the result of the deception of Rebekah for herself? For Esau? For Jacob?

9. The name Jacob means "Deceiver." Do you think he inherited this trait of character, or did he learn this from his mother? Do you think that Jews generally display this characteristic in their business dealings?

5. Jacob's Spiritual Wrestling
Genesis 32:22-32

1. A man wrestled with Jacob; in Hosea 12:3, 4 we read that he wrestled with God and that an Angel wrestled with him. How can a man wrestle with God?

2. Jacob was very anxious, evidently due to his guilt feelings. Why do guilt feelings bring anxiety?

3. Jacob was alone. Why are some people afraid to be alone? How can we overcome that feeling?

4. Jacob first prayed earnestly, then he provided for his family and sent a gift to Esau. Was this a good idea? Was it not enough just to pray to God for help? Was he not trying to help God along a bit?

5. Jacob first wrestled in his human strength. What does this show us about his character?

6. When Jacob was crippled by the touch of the angel, he began his spiritual wrestling. What is spiritual wrestling? Can we do this today? Should we?

7. How do people fight against God? Why do they do this since they know they can't win?

8. Why did God give Jacob a new name?

9. Do you think it is correct to call this experience at the Jabbok Jacob's conversion experience?

10. What was the secret of victory for Jacob? For us?

11. Jacob was a cripple the rest of his life. If he genuinely turned to God, why did God not heal him? Does this show that God punishes him? Would this indicate that even though he was a true believer he still had to suffer for his sins? Is this true today also?

6. Joseph—The Dreamer
Genesis 37:1-11

1. Do you think it was right for Joseph to bring an evil report to his father about his brothers? How should we deal with children who tattle on their brothers and sisters?

2. Jacob seemed to favor Joseph because he was a son of his favorite wife and he was born in his old age. Do you think parents tend to favor the youngest child, especially one that is born some years after the next oldest one?

3. Do you think parents can treat each child alike, or do they usually favor one over another? Do you think your parents treated all their children alike?

4. Joseph dreamed and then talked about his dreams. Do you think dreams are significant today? Was God speaking in a special way through Joseph's dreams? Does He still do that today?

5. Do you think Joseph's brothers were correct when they felt that their youngest brother was proud? What is the difference between being proud and having a healthy sense of self-confidence?

6. Do you like Joseph?

7. Jacob's sons intended to kill Joseph. What do you think of Reuben's remarks in verses 21 and 22? Was he really doing Joseph a favor?

8. The root of the evil of Jacob's sons was envy, and it led to selling their brother into slavery. Are any of us free from envy?

9. Were the brothers of Joseph guilty of murder?

10. How does this story indicate that "all things work together for good"? How can something that is evil turn out for good? Does the end justify the means? See Genesis 50:19, 20.

7. Jacob—Feeling Sorry for Himself
Genesis 42:29-38

1. Jacob says, "All things are against me." Do you think he was feeling sorry for himself? Notice that none of the things he worried about were true.

2. Is there a difference between feeling sorry for oneself and developing a martyr complex?

3. A wife says, "I work my fingers to the bone, and no one seems to appreciate it." What's wrong with her? Or is there something wrong with her family?

4. How does a person develop the habit of feeling sorry for himself?

5. Is it a good thing for parents to remind their children of all the sacrifices they have made for them?

6. Some people often feel they are unjustly criticized for something they do. Why do they react this way?

7. Sometimes people who have lived a successful life get a heart attack, or some other illness, and from then on they feel that everyone must treat them gently. Why?

8. Do you think that when patients leave a hospital they should expect that people are going to treat them with a little special consideration?

9. Is it good to remind a person that he is feeling sorry for himself?

10. How can we overcome a martyr complex?

11. "The man who is indulging in self-pity is not facing up to life, but he is running away from it." Is this true?

12. Did Jacob get over his self-pity? How? Read Genesis 48:15-16.

8. Miriam—A Case of Envy
Numbers 12:1-15

1. In Micah 6:4 we read, "I sent before thee Moses, Aaron and Miriam." They were the three leaders of Israel.

2. At the Red Sea Miriam appears as a leader of the people in song. It seems that she was a career woman. Do you think it is good for a woman to seek a career rather than marriage?

3. In Numbers 12 we read of her envy. Do you think she had a good reason for being jealous or envious? At the beginning of the chapter she gives her reason for this. Do you think this was the real reason? Do people usually give the real reasons for their feelings, or are these "reasons" merely excuses?

4. Was it right for Moses to marry a dark-skinned woman, one who was not a Jewess?

5. Don't you think that Aaron and Miriam had some good reasons for feeling jealous and envious of Moses? Did he not take too much authority for himself?

6. Why would the Lord punish Miriam instead of Aaron, or both of them? Is this part of the Jewish tradition that women are not as important as men?

7. Notice how Moses handled the envious feelings of Miriam. How should we handle our own feelings of envy?

8. Do you think that women are more inclined to be jealous and envious than men? Do you think that women are inclined to be jealous of men?

9. Children often show a lot of rivalry and jealousy among themselves in the home. Psychologists call this "sibling rivalry." Is this something serious? How does it affect our mental health? What must we do about it as parents?

10. Adolescents often have tremendous rivalries about boy-friends or girl-friends. Is this good or bad? What can you do about it?

9. Balaam—The Inconsistent
Numbers 23:1-10

1. This is a strange story. Do you think it is true that the ass really spoke to Balaam? Could he not have imagined this?

2. Balaam was a prophet of God, yet a servant of evil. In Numbers 23:10 he says that he would like to die the death of the righteous, but he does not live such a life. Can you find examples of such inconsistency today?

3. An elder in the church may drive a hard bargain in his business. Some people are pleasant when others are around, but hard to live with in their own families. What is wrong with people who are extremely inconsistent?

4. When a person acts like two different people we see that he divides life into little compartments. What is wrong with compartmentalization? What are its dangers?

5. Do our doctrine and life ever fully agree? Do we ever fully practice what we preach?

6. In what way is the person who worries too much an inconsistent person?

7. How can we develop greater consistency in our lives? Is this a matter of the Christian faith, or a matter of character and personality?

8. Is there such a person as a consistent Christian?

9. What must be the one thing that unifies all of our life?

10. Would you say that an unbeliever is always an inconsistent person?

11. In Matthew 6:33 we read about a wonderful means of finding unity in our lives.

10. Caleb—Ready to Be in the Minority
Joshua 14

1. Caleb is one of the finest men of the Old Testament. He was a Kenezite, brought into the Jewish nation. Does this possibly explain his devotion to God?

2. He was ready to be in the minority. Why are so few people ready to be in a minority group? The word *minority group* is often used unfavorably today. Why?

3. Why were the people of Israel more ready to believe the bad news than the good news? Is this still true today?

4. God says of Caleb—and Caleb's life confirms this—that "he wholly followed the Lord." What does this mean?

5. Why is it important to have something that unifies our life? What effect does this have on a person's life? What are some of the things that tend to divide our life and interests?

6. A doctor writes, "The great sickness of our age is aimlessness, boredom and lack of purpose in living." Do you think this is true? In what sense is it true among us?

7. Caleb in his old age went out to conquer the Anakim. How do you explain this kind of vigor in a man of eighty-five? Do you think that Caleb bore a grudge against the Anakim for all of the forty-five years?

11. Deborah—The Prophetess
Judges 4

1. Deborah was a very influential woman in the land of Israel. What was the strength she manifested? Was this due to the fact that she was a prophetess, or that she had a strong personality, or both?

2. Since Deborah did the work of a prophet in those days, why don't we have women preachers today? Should we have women in our consistories?

3. Would it be good to have a woman as President of the United States some day?

4. What do you think of Barak who would not go out to fight unless Deborah went along into the battle? Is he something like the man who would not go to the dentist unless his wife went with him to hold his hand?

5. In the battle against Sisera and his army, the Lord sent rain and an earthquake and a swollen river. God did not really need the army of Barak. Why does God make use of means? Why does God make use of means today, such as medicine or treatments to give healing in sickness? What must be our attitude toward the use of means?

6. Jael is often presented as a cruel and deceptive woman. What do you think? Was the thing she did a womanly thing to do? Do we expect different actions from men than we do from women?

7. Do you think women are taking over positions and lines of work that really belong to men?

12. Gideon—A Battle without Weapons
Judges 6:11-15; 7:1-7

1. In Judges 6:13 Gideon asks the question "why." Is it always wrong to ask this question? What is wrong with Gideon's attitude when he asks this question? Is it not good to look into the past to see why things are as they are today?

2. What is God's answer to Gideon's question? What help does that answer give?

3. Did Gideon have an inferiority complex? 6:15. Was this a good approach?

4. When the army of Israel was gathered together there were thirty-two thousand men. Of these, twenty-two thousand were afraid and went home. Were these men cowards? Does this not seem like a high percentage of "scared people"? Do you think the percentage is better today?

5. Why did God feel that ten thousand men made up too large an army? Why did God choose to fight with only three hundred men? Is there any advantage in having a small group work for a given cause?

6. One of the reasons for the success of the Billy Graham campaigns is the fact that there is strength in large organizations, big crowds, etc. Is this contrary to the idea of Gideon's band?

7. Gideon wanted a sign from God. Is it wrong to look for signs today? Would it not be easier to believe that God hears our prayers if we had more visible indications?

8. Do you think the method used to select the three hundred men was important?

9. Who gained the victory for Israel—the army of Gideon or the hand of the Lord?

10. When we fight life's battles are the weapons that we use of any importance? Gideon's torches and trumpets were hardly adequate means to conquer a large army. Should we use the best means that are available to us?

13. Samson—Playing with Sin
Judges 16:15-31

1. Though Samson was a Nazarite, he had many of the qualities of an overgrown boy. Why could a person in his position take such a playful attitude toward life?

2. Do you feel that having great physical strength is conducive to godliness? How about physical beauty?

3. Did Samson make any spiritual contributions during the time he ruled as judge?

4. Samson often made use of revenge and anger. Is this good?

5. Samson was a strong man but he was overcome by a clever woman. How can women influence men for good, or for evil? Do you think women can still control men by their feminine charms? Should they?

6. Samson played with temptation. Is it wrong for a person to allow himself to be tempted, if he is confident that he can resist temptations?

7. Was Samson's temptation the work of Satan, or did the temptations come out of his own sinful heart and sinful desires? What is the difference? Can we ever blame Satan for our temptations?

8. Samson was blinded and placed in prison. Was this a punishment from God? Does God ever punish people in this way? Would this be chastisement?

9. What is the relationship between sin and sickness in our day? Is it punishment, chastisement, or is God just testing us?

10. Do you think Samson was converted in prison?

11. Did Samson commit suicide when he pulled down the pillars of the Temple of Dagon?

12. In Hebrews 11 Samson was counted among the heroes of faith. How do you explain this?

14. Ruth and Naomi—A Living Testimony
Ruth 1

1. Naomi and Elimelech departed to Moab in time of famine. Was it wrong for them to do this? Is it wrong to move our families into an unchurched area for the sake of better economic conditions?

2. Are mixed marriages always wrong? When can and should they be approved?

3. Naomi argued with her daughters-in-law, telling them they should stay in Moab. Why did she do this? Do you think she really wanted them to go back? What do you think of this kind of Christian testimony?

4. What was the difference between Orpah and Ruth?

5. In Ruth's confession it seems as though she was greatly influenced by Naomi. She wanted to stay with her mother-in-law, even though she knew the price. Was this faith in God, or just love for Naomi? Can we separate those two?

6. Naomi means "pleasantness;" Mara means "bitterness." Do you think that Naomi's remark, "Call me Mara" was an expression of faith, or of depression? Did she not seem to look too much at the dark side of life?

7. Ruth became one of the ancestors of Christ. Why are there people of heathen origin among His ancestors?

8. What is the most important kind of witness and testimony—that of words or that of a life?

9. The Book of Ruth is a love story, the love and marriage of Ruth and Boaz. What are some of the things that it teaches us about courtship and marriage? Do you think that our present practices in dating, engagement and marriage are the best ones? How could they be improved?

15. Eli—A Permissive Parent
I Samuel 2:18-26

1. Eli was a rather permissive father in his dealings with his sons. How do you feel about this approach to the training of children? What are some of the advantages of a more permissive attitude?

2. Should children learn because they have to, or should we make our education and training so interesting that children want to learn?

3. Can parents be too strict in the training of their youngsters? How can you tell whether you are too soft, or too strict?

4. It is said that if parents make all the decisions for their children, children will never be able to make decisions for themselves. What do you think? Should you allow a little child to choose the dress or shirt that should be worn for the day? How about choice of food?

5. Should children be spanked? When is a youngster too old to be spanked? Can children be spanked too much?

6. How do you feel about a parent who says he will allow his son to make a choice of religion or church when he reaches that age, rather than to make this choice for him at an early age?

7. Should parents control the length of hair for a high-school boy, or the length of a skirt for a high-school girl?

8. How much influence may parents exert in the choice of a mate for children as they grow up? How can you do this?

9. Should children be given an allowance that they can spend for themselves, or should they always ask their parents for money to buy the things the parents approve?

10. The story of Eli shows the danger of permissiveness in the home. What is the real danger of this today? Do you feel a child in a permissive home is really secure? Do children appreciate permissive parents or teachers?

16. David—The Cost of Friendship
I Samuel 20:17-23; II Samuel 1:23-27

1. What are some of the basic ingredients of friendship? Do you think a husband and wife should be friends? What about parents and children?

2. When a couple has been "going steady" and then decides to be "just friends" what does this mean?

3. Why do people need friends? Some people say that they haven't a friend in the world. What is wrong?

4. Some people say that their church is unfriendly. Is this the fault of the church or the individual? Why do some churches seem to be more friendly than others? What can members do to make a church more friendly?

5. When you move into a new community, how can you go about making new friends?

6. In high schools and churches there are often "little cliques." Is this good or bad?

7. Children often find it hard to establish enduring friendships. How can parents help them in this area?

8. Is it permissible for married people to have friends of the opposite sex? Should all friendships of married people be friends of both husband and wife, or can there be "your friends" and "my friends"?

9. What are some of the hazards of having very close friends?

17. Elijah—A Depressed Prophet
I Kings 19:1-18

1. Elijah had just experienced a day of triumph at Mount Carmel. Now he must run for his life. Do you think this can account for his depressed feelings?

2. Is his feeling of failure the cause or the result of his depressed feelings?

3. Where was his faith at this time? Is lack of trust the cause or the result of depressed feelings?

4. What do you think of his request to die? Is it wrong to pray a prayer like this. Was it selfish?

5. God did not grant his request. In what way did He give him something better? Was this an unanswered prayer?

6. Why did God feed Elijah at this time? Can his physical exhaustion explain his depressed feelings?

7. Do you think that depression as we see it today is something emotional, or is it physical, or is it spiritual?

8. Does this passage give us any remedy for depression?

9. Several of the great men of the Bible suffered from periods of doubt (David, John the Baptist, Paul). Do you feel that this indicates that there are highs and lows in our faith? Why does the Lord allow this to happen?

18. Naaman—The Leper
II Kings 5:1-19

1. Naaman was an important man, but he was a leper. Since sickness is no respecter of persons, how do you feel about publicizing the sicknesses and aches of our national leaders?

2. One of the finest characters in this story is the little captive girl. Do you think children can have a strong faith, or was this a rather naive kind of faith? Do you think children are more tolerant than adults?

3. Naaman goes to the wrong place for healing, with the wrong prince, the wrong attitude and the wrong prescription. In what way do we often make the same mistakes he did?

4. The wise servant gives his master good advice. Why do people find it so hard to accept advice?

5. Why do people fail so often when it comes to little things but are quite ready to face big or difficult things?

6. Was the healing of Naaman like our modern faith healing?

7. Why did Elijah refuse to accept the handsome fee that was offered by Naaman? Does this imply that ministers should not accept fees for special services?

8. When Naaman leaves for home he takes with him some of the soil of Palestine to make a shrine for the worship of God. Did he become a believer in Jehovah? Did Elijah give him permission to continue to worship Rimmon?

9. Naaman was a materialist. What is wrong with materialism? Do you think we are guilty of it? How can you overcome it?

19. Gehazi—The Thief
II Kings 5:20-27

1. Gehazi has the privilege of being a personal servant of a great prophet. How would you explain the fact that he became the kind of person he was? Ministers' children have a reputation for being worse than other children. Why? Are they really worse?

2. Gehazi's sin begins with a desire to have some of the riches of Naaman. Does sin always begin with desire? Is it true that we first think a sin before we carry out the act?

3. Do you think Gehazi was a clever liar? Can a person ever tell a convincing lie?

4. Why was the sin of Gehazi considered to be such a serious one?

5. When children cheat in school, they are being dishonest. Do you think there is less cheating among children of Christian families than children of non-Christian people?

6. How can we help our children to be more honest in their school work? How should we deal with a youngster that is caught cheating?

7. Shoplifting is becoming a problem in our society today. Why should this develop at a time when economic conditions are favorable? What can be done about it? What should you do if your child would be involved in an act of pilfering from a store?

8. Do you think the punishment of Gehazi was too severe, considering the crime he had committed?

9. Do you feel that Gehazi showed a character weakness, or did he just fall into sin? What is the difference between the two?

10. Was there forgiveness for a man like Gehazi?

20. Elisha's Servant—Seeing the Unseen
II Kings 6:8-19

1. The servant of Elisha first saw only the things that are seen—the dangers. How would you answer the man who says that only the things that are seen are real?

2. In what way are we also in danger of seeing only the visible things, and not the invisible?

3. In what way does God give spiritual vision to the servant of Elisha? Does this still work today?

4. What were "the horses and chariots of fire" that they saw? Were these angels? Does God still protect His people by means of angels today? Do you think each person has a guardian angel?

5. If you told your psychiatrist that you saw a vision like the one in this story, he might think you were having delusions. What is the difference?

6. What was the effect of seeing these unseen forces?

7. Do you think that Elisha was deceitful when he led the Syrian army into Samaria?

8. What lesson did he teach the people about their attitude toward their enemies? Must we love our enemies today, or is there also room for some hate?

21. Esther—An Example of Courage
Esther 4:9-17

1. Esther won her position as queen in a form of beauty contest. Do you think a Christian girl should enter the Miss America contest?

2. Mordecai placed Esther before a difficult choice. Why do some people find it so hard to make decisions? What can be done about this?

3. Esther displayed courage. There are two kinds of courage: some people seem to face danger with recklessness and lack of fear; others are afraid, and yet they move ahead to face danger. Which of these two shows the greater courage?

4. How can parents help their children to face dangers and difficulties with greater courage?

5. Some people are afraid of the dark, or of an electric storm, or of riding in an airplane. How do people develop such fears, and how can they overcome them?

6. How can we learn to overcome the ordinary fears of life?

7. Do you think the Christian faith helps us to overcome fears? Should we try to overcome all our fears?

8. When Esther said, "If I perish, I perish," was this a display of courage or was she just blindly accepting the inevitable?

9. What is the difference between courage and recklessness? Is the modern hero of the Western T.V. dramas a good illustration of courage?

10. Do you think Esther used her feminine appeal to good advantage? Do you think it proper for a wife to use such appeals to influence her husband?

11. Since the name of God is not mentioned in the Book of Esther, does the book have a place in the Bible? Why was it placed there?

22. Daniel—Making a Good Choice
Daniel 1:8-16

1. Daniel and his friends were faced with a strange choice. Don't you think they were being a bit fussy when they refused to eat the king's food?

2. What effect will our early training have on our ability to make choices?

3. On what basis did these young men make their choice? Is this still the basis for our choices today?

4. If you find it difficult to select a shirt or dress in a store, is it good to have someone help you make the decision, or is it better to learn to make your own choices? What is the danger of indecision?

5. Some people make up their minds to do a certain thing and then they refuse to change. Is this being stubborn? Is this good?

6. When we make a choice that is contrary to one which most other people make, does this show that we are wrong? How can you tell? Is it good to be in the minority?

7. Should we choose with our intellect, or with our feelings, or both? What is the difference?

8. If we make a wrong decision, what must we do about it?

9. These three men in Babylon showed real courage. How do people develop that kind of courage? Is making a good decision a part of developing courage?

10. When we make our spiritual commitment to Christ how will this influence our choices in life?

23. Jonah—Running Away from God
Jonah 1

1. Jonah was a prophet of God. God called him to go to Nineveh, a nation that was hostile to Israel. Do you think God still calls people in this way? Does He call a minister to go to a certain church, or does a minister accept a call for personal reasons?

2. Jonah refused to go. The reason he gave was that he was afraid Nineveh might repent. Are there still people like that today? Is this narrow-mindedness?

3. There are many people who take flight from duty at times. Can you illustrate how we do this today?

4. Why do people make use of alcohol or drugs to escape facing up to life?

5. Is trying to run away from our problems always a case of running away from God? Or are we merely trying to get away from ourselves?

6. Do you think people ever use a convenient headache or stomach-ache to get away from life's demands? How can we overcome this?

7. People will often use excuses for staying away from church, or for not being active in the church. Is there such a thing as a good excuse?

8. What happens to the person who tries to run away from God, or from the pathway of duty?

9. Why could Jonah sleep so comfortably in the hold of the ship when all the sailors were so afraid? Can a person who is running away from God still feel that God will take care of him?

10. Was Jonah really swallowed by a whale?

11. Jonah was disgusted when the city of Nineveh repented from sin. Do you think people today are happy to see sinners repent? Do you feel that your church is ready to accept a repentant sinner?

24. Handling Our Tensions
Psalm 37:1-11

1. Why is there so much tension among us today when we actually have things easier and more comfortable than our grandparents did?

2. Do you think people are busier today than their parents or grandparents were? Or do we just have a busyness complex?

3. Is it a good thing to schedule our work and then try to live within a schedule?

4. For some people a hobby is relaxing, for others it seems to build up tension. How can you make a hobby a real form of relaxation?

5. Why does going to church make some people tense? Should church attendance build up tension?

6. How should our Christian faith help us to relieve our tensions? In verse 2 David says, "Trust in Jehovah." If we had enough faith in God would we still suffer from tensions?

7. In verse 4 we are told to "Delight thyself in Jehovah." How can this help us conquer the conflicting desires we have?

8. In verse 5 we are reminded to "Commit thy way unto Jehovah." Do you think a person who is emotionally troubled can really do this? How is this done?

9. Verse 7 tells us to "rest in Jehovah." In what way can this give us peace of heart and mind?

10. If a person followed all these instructions of David, could he still suffer from emotional or mental illness?

11. How do you feel about a person who tells you to go to Christ instead of a psychiatrist or to "pray instead of using tranquilizers"?

25. Do We Worship Idols?
Psalm 115

1. The Bible often condemns idolatry. What is idolatry? Do you think there is idolatry among us today?

2. Money is called "mammon" in the Bible. In what way is the search after riches idolatry? When does money become a god?

3. Why do some people who have been poor change for the worse when they gain a measure of wealth?

4. Do you think a person can be a better Christian if he is poor, of average means, or rich?

5. Pleasure, or the search after it, is often described as another form of idolatry. In which way is it?

6. Many people contrast work and pleasure. A person finishes his work and says, "Now I can enjoy myself." What do you think about that attitude?

7. Do you think that a Christian could be a professional entertainer? Are any of the entertainers consecrated Christians?

8. "We have become a people who do not know the art of finding individual enjoyment and we must be entertained by others." Is this healthy?

9. Where should a Christian find pleasure? Is it wrong to watch a humorous program on T.V.? To read the comic strips in the newspaper?

10. The desire for status is often described as being part of modern idolatry. Do you think it is?

11. What is wrong with trying to "keep up with the Joneses"?

12. It is not wrong to try to get ahead in life. Why then is status-seeking wrong?

13. What is the remedy for modern idolatries?

26. Taking a Positive Attitude
Psalm 119:9-16

1. Some people seem to enjoy expressing their opposition to any change that is suggested. They often say, "It's always been that way." What is wrong with such people? Why do people have a need to be so negative?

2. Many parents use many more "don'ts" than "do's" in training their children. What effect will this have on the family? Can parents also be afraid of being too negative?

3. A negative critic or faultfinder can do more to break down a cause or organization than what many people can do to build one up. Do such critics also make a good contribution? Is it good to have an opposition party in government?

4. There are many protest groups in our country, such as the anti-communist or anti-segregationist groups. Is it a good thing to become involved in such protest groups?

5. Some churches have rules such as "don't smoke; don't play cards; don't dance; don't drink." Do you think it is good for a church or a school to use such negative approaches? Would it not be better to be more positive?

6. Do you think it helps to "think positively" about some problem, or about our work?

7. What is wrong with the person who has become too negative in life? Can the Christian faith help us become more positive?

8. May a Christian be a pessimist? Is it possible always to be an optimist?

9. Psalm 119:9 asks, "Wherewith shall a young man cleanse his way?" This is answered, "Thy word have I hid in my heart." Does this really work?

10. How can we "overcome evil with good"? Romans 12:10.

27. Our Attitudes toward Work
Proverbs 6:6-11

1. Solomon uses the illustration of the ant to tell us about the folly of being lazy. Do you think there are many lazy people today?

2. A man says, "I just work in a factory," or a woman says, "I'm just a housewife." What is wrong with this kind of attitude toward work?

3. Why do some people rebel at unpleasant work? How can we learn to accept the fact that every job has some unpleasant things about it?

4. Do you think that labor unions have had a good influence on the laboring man's attitude toward his work?

5. Some people take a spirit of resignation toward their work: "You can't do anything about it anyway; you might as well accept it." Is this a good attitude toward our daily work?

6. What would you consider to be an ideal job?

7. What incentives can we find that will give us a better attitude toward our work?

8. Do you think that good pay is a sufficient incentive to promote a healthy attitude toward our work?

9. How do you feel about the regulations of the government that forbid discrimination between men and women in a given field of work? Do you feel that a woman should receive equal pay for equal work?

10. Do you think that it is a Christian requirement to save some of the money that is earned?

11. Do you feel that the support that is given by the state for the unemployed encourages people to be less diligent in their work? Does it tend to make people lazy?

12. Should a father take a job that requires that he regularly works the night shift? What are the dangers of irregular hours of work in family living?

28. Controlled by Others
Proverbs 15:1-9

1. Why do most people resent having other people "boss them"? Is this good or bad?

2. Is there anyone in the world who can truthfully say that he is his own boss so that he can do as he pleases?

3. Some people are controlled by their own thoughts. How can we learn to conquer these controlling thoughts when they are not wholesome for us?

4. Some people are slaves to food, others to drink, some to other bad habits. Can we conquer such slavery?

5. How can a person conquer his own base feelings, such as anger, jealousy, hostility, envy, etc.?

6. What is the meaning of self-denial as mentioned by Jesus in Matthew 16:24? How can we learn this?

7. Why is self-discipline important in a person's life? Does this have anything to do with our mental health?

8. Do you think our churches and schools tend to teach people self-control, or do they tend to make people more dependent?

9. Do our spiritual resources help us learn to master ourselves? How?

10. Is it good to allow others to control us, or must we control ourselves?

29. Learning Self-control
Proverbs 16:25-33

1. Some people find it hard to control their feelings of resentment or anger, while others do a good job of controlling them. Why is there this difference in people?

2. How can we learn to control our tempers?

3. A person may make an unkind remark about us. Some people get quite upset about this. Why?

4. When some people experience long periods of serious illness, or sorrow, they find it hard to control their feelings of disappointment or grief. How should we learn to control ourselves in these experiences?

5. Some people repress their feelings, pushing them into the background and trying to forget about them. Is this a good way to handle our feelings?

6. Do you think that our childhood has an important influence on the measure of self-control we develop? How can we help our children in this way?

7. Do you think the Christian faith can be of help in learning greater self-control? How?

8. Does anyone ever learn complete self-control?

9. What is wrong with the kind of person who never becomes angry or feels resentment?

10. Jesus gives us a beautiful example of self-control. How should we follow His example?

THE SERMON ON THE MOUNT

30. The Poor in Spirit

(Matthew 5:3)

Matthew 5:1-12

The Beatitudes do not describe eight kinds of people, but they present traits of character that should be found in every Christian. They present qualities quite different from the standards of the world.

1. To be poor in spirit refers to those who are conscious of their sins. Is it also possible to think too little of ourselves?

2. Is it good to compare ourselves with others so that we can state that we are "better than some, worse than others, and just as good as the rest"?

3. Paul calls himself the chief of sinners. Is this a good way to be thinking about ourselves?

4. Is a Christian still totally depraved?

5. Why does Jesus condemn so strongly the spirit of self-righteousness? Why is a self-righteous person so hard to live with?

6. Some people feel they are such great sinners they should not partake of the Lord's Supper. What is wrong with this approach? Do you think there are times when we feel our sinfulness to such an extent that it would be better not to partake?

7. There is a tendency among people to say they are great sinners, but if you ask them to mention ten of their sins they can't do it. Why is this so?

8. The Heidelberg Catechism lays a great deal of emphasis on the greatness of our sin. Wouldn't it be better to lay more emphasis on the marvel of the grace of God? Don't you feel this is a rather negative approach?

9. The poor in spirit are assured the kingdom of heaven. Is this something only for the future, or does it also have meaning for the present?

31. Blessed Mourners

(Matthew 5:4)

John 14:1-11

1. Some people find real satisfaction in this Beatitude and use it as an excuse for a glum or gloomy outlook on life. What is wrong with such an attitude? Can we do anything about it if we have such a tendency?

2. Others mourn by feeling sorry for themselves. How do people develop such an attitude? How does one get over it?

3. Jesus referred to mourning over sin. Do we mourn because of sin, or because of the results of sin? How can we distinguish between the two?

4. Why do some people grieve for a long time over the loss of a loved one? How can we conquer grief?

5. In our world there are many things to be deeply concerned about, such as war, crime, immorality, and the sad state of religion. Is it good to mourn about such things?

6. Why is it blessed to mourn?

7. True comfort means that we receive something that will help us overcome our grief. What is that gift that the Lord gives?

8. Will "thinking positively" help us overcome a gloomy disposition?

9. If we truly mourn about our sins, will this always lead to an assurance of forgiveness?

10. There has been a lot of emphasis on "peace of heart" and "peace of mind." Is this good? Don't you think it would be better if people shed a few tears now and then? Is there too much complacency about sin?

32. Blessed Are the Meek

(Matthew 5:5)

Colossians 3:12-17

1. Webster defines meekness as being patient, mild and not inclined to anger. Do you think a meek person would make a good husband or wife?

2. Moses is described as being "very meek." When he was younger he seemed to be rather quick tempered. What made him change?

3. Do you think people are born meek, or do they learn to be meek?

4. What kind of discipline is required to develop meekness? Do you think sickness helps?

5. Can a person be too meek, so that he becomes a very passive personality? How do people develop that quality?

6. Why are many people so easily provoked by little things, when often the bigger things of life are accepted with more calmness?

7. Someone writes that "they that mourn" refers to a person's attitude toward God, while "meekness" refers to our attitude toward our fellow-men. What do you think of this?

8. Is it true that the meek inherit the earth? Does it not rather seem that the bold and the arrogant rule the world?

9. What is the meaning of living victoriously? Does this imply that we shall always prosper?

10. How can sickness or sorrow be for us a "creative experience"?

11. Two brothers were in a business venture that failed. The one brother took what he could salvage, moved away, and prospered financially. The other spent many years of his life to pay the debts they had incurred. Which of these two faced life victoriously?

33. Hungering after Righteousness

(Matthew 5:6)

Matthew 5:38-48

1. Two aspects of righteousness are found in the Bible: a righteousness of the heart and a righteousness of our lives. The first means to be right with God, the second is revealed in the way we live.

2. Is it necessary that we have a conversion experience to be right with God? Do you think that persons who have a dramatic or sudden conversion experience have an advantage over those who gradually came to the awareness that they were children of God? Why?

3. What is the ideal age for profession of faith?

4. "Hungering and thirsting" indicate a very strong craving. Why is this often lacking in our spiritual life?

5. Is it blessed to "hunger" or is the real blessing in being "filled"?

6. There should also be a strong desire to be righteous in our lives. May we ever feel that we are "pretty good Christians"? Should we always be dissatisfied with ourselves?

7. Is it possible to set our goals too high in our spiritual life?

8. What is wrong with perfectionism?

9. Sometimes people say about children that they are "too good," or that they should get into mischief once in a while. What do you think of this?

10. Most people are satisfied when they live as good as the average people they associate with. Is this a good way to live? People usually do not like those who live above or below the average. Why?

11. What does it mean "they shall be filled"? Is that in this life or in the life to come?

34. Christian Mercy

(Matthew 5:7)

Luke 10:25-37

1. Mercy implies kindness, sympathy and compassion to others in distress. It seems that some persons are more merciful than others. Can everyone learn to be merciful?

2. Why should a Christian be merciful?

3. Is benevolence or sympathy a matter of an attitude that we take to others, or does it mean doing something for others?

4. The good Samaritan is an example of real compassion. Is it necessary to go out of our way at our own expense to show mercy as he did? Don't you think he carried things a bit too far?

5. Can a non-Christian be merciful?

6. The word *mercy* also implies that we are willing to forgive others the wrongs they have done to us. How far must we go with this? If a marriage partner is unfaithful to us, must we still be ready to forgive?

7. How do you feel about the general term that is used to describe our hospitals as "institutions of mercy"? Do you think that nurses should be called "angels of mercy"?

8. Should parents show mercy to their children or to each other? How?

9. Do you think the race riots show a lack of mercy and compassion?

10. What does it mean to help others "in His name"?

11. In our churches the office of Christian mercy is established in the deacons. Do you think the church is really interested in helping its fellow-members?

12. Is not this Beatitude a bit selfish since it states that if we are merciful we shall receive mercy? Does not this imply that you give help to others because someday you yourself may need help?

35. The Pure in Heart

(Matthew 5:8)

Philippians 4:1-9

1. The word *pure* as used here refers to something that is genuine, like pure gold—something that is clean or unstained. Are the pure in heart perfect?

2. Don't you think people often put up a front to give the impression that they are better than they really are? Is this being a hypocrite?

3. Can our thoughts ever be pure? Is it true that sin always begins in the thoughts, or are there also thoughtless sins?

4. How can we control our thoughts? Our imaginations?

5. Is it just as wrong to have an impure or hostile thought as to express these thoughts in actions?

6. "No man is ever as good as his creed." Is this true?

7. Do you think that modern literature, drama on T.V., etc. tends to have an influence on our thoughts?

8. How can we keep our thoughts from wandering to other things when we are engaged in prayer or worship?

9. In what way does the Christian faith help us to be purer in heart?

10. What does it mean that the pure in heart shall "see God"? Is this only in the life to come, or also in this life?

36. The Peace-makers

(Matthew 5:9)

Matthew 18:15-22

1. The world has always needed peace-makers, because there is so much strife and war. There is much hatred and envy even among Christian people. Why do you think there is so much hostility in the lives of people—even Christian people?

2. There are some people with whom you just can't pick a quarrel or start an argument. Are these people peace-makers?

3. Should we seek for peace at any price? Or are there times when we should not have peace?

4. Often when we try to reconcile two people who are quarreling, they both become angry at us. Why is this so?

5. Some peace-loving people seem to be wishy-washy types of personality. Is this the true Christian spirit?

6. Does Jesus here refer only to making peace between men, or also between God and men?

7. Can we do anything to help promote world peace?

8. The peace-makers are called "sons of God." Why?

9. If we have trouble with other people, how must we try to bring peace again? If others have offended us or hurt us, is it our duty to talk to them about this, or should we wait till they come to see us?

10. In Matthew 18:15-17 Jesus tells us how to deal with those with whom we have had some clash. Why don't people use this method more?

11. Wouldn't it be better if Jesus had said, "Blessed are those that never get into trouble with their fellow-men"?

37. The Christian's Persecution

(Matthew 5:10-12)

Matthew 5:1-12

1. Do you feel that some people think they are being persecuted, while actually they have a martyr complex? What is the difference?

2. Why do people dislike Christians and cause them to suffer? Is it possible that some Christians give occasion for being disliked?

3. Is there much persecution today? Why? Don't you think that in a land like ours people are too tolerant of the other man's religion?

4. A man lost his job because he refused to work on Sunday. Is this persecution?

5. Some men refuse to go along with the practice of certain labor unions because of their Christian principles. As a result they do not receive the promotions to which they are entitled. Is this persecution?

6. Often when a member of a Jewish family accepts Christ he is rejected by the rest of the family. Is this persecution?

7. Don't you think we would be better Christians if we had to endure more of the scorn and ridicule of the non-Christian world?

8. Luke says, "Woe unto you if all men speak well of you." What does this mean? May a Christian try to be popular? Do you think a popular minister can be more effective than one who is unpopular?

9. There have been people who were called upon to die for their faith in Christ, such as the five missionaries who went to the Auca Indians. Some people feel they needlessly endangered their lives. What do you think? What qualities of character are required to give ourselves sacrificially for Christ?

10. Why is it blessed to be persecuted?

38. Going the Second Mile
Matthew 5:38-48

1. The tendency among many people is to live just "average" lives. Is this a good attitude toward life? Should we be satisfied if our marriage is just as good as the "average"?

2. Often when people try to be better than the average in society, people will not like them. They feel that they are "stuck-up." Why is this so?

3. Jesus tells us to "be perfect." If we would do this would we not be perfectionists? What is wrong with perfectionism?

4. It is often said that it is better for children to be average students than to get straight "A's." How do you feel about this?

5. Is it possible to set our standards too high in our work? In the Christian life?

6. In this passage Jesus tells us to be willing to go beyond the demands of duty for our fellow-men. Should we treat others better than we do ourselves?

7. Why is it so hard for us to "turn the other cheek" when we deal with our fellow-men?

8. Do you think the church goes the second mile in the way it deals with the race question? In the attitude toward other churches?

9. How was Jesus an example of one who went beyond the second mile?

39. Facing Up to Reality
Matthew 6:24-34

1. There is a little prayer that is often quoted:

God, give me the serenity
to accept the things I cannot change;
The courage to change the things I can;
And the wisdom to know the difference.

What is your personal reaction to this prayer?

2. Sometimes patients come to a hospital who have very difficult experiences at home, things that cannot very easily be changed. What can treatment at a hospital do for such people?

3. Some people escape from facing reality by fantasy—imagining that things are not so bad after all. Is this good or bad?

4. How do you feel about the person who meekly bows under the load of life and says, "If it's the Lord's will, I'll just suffer it patiently"?

5. How should we teach our children to face up to the reality of life? Should they be made aware of the fact that there are such things as serious illnesses and death?

6. Children go through a great deal of day-dreaming. The girl dreams of marrying a handsome man. The boy dreams of being a fireman or a big-league pitcher. Should this be discouraged?

7. Do you think that some people go to a mental hospital in order to avoid facing the hard realities of life? Should the hospital encourage this?

8. Must a Christian be a realist, or an idealist?

9. How can we face the realities of life in a victorious way?

10. What are some of the suggestions Jesus gives to help us face life as found in the Scripture passage?

40. The Habit of Faultfinding
Matthew 7:1-6

1. Jesus teaches the evil of faultfinding by means of a story that has a bit of humor in it. Did Jesus laugh? Do you think a minister today should spice up his sermons with a bit of humor?

2. What is the difference between faultfinding and criticism?

3. Does Jesus teach here that we may never criticize others as long as we have faults in our life?

4. Why do some people become angry whenever they are criticized? Why do some people become discouraged when criticized?

5. How can faultfinding be an expression of our own feelings of inferiority?

6. Someone has written, "We often find fault with others because we recognize their sins due to the fact that we have the same ones." Is this true? If it is, why do we criticize others?

7. "You can find in the lives of others the things you are looking for. If you look for the worst you will be sure to find it; if you look for the best you will also find this." What does this tell us about the habit of faultfinding? Give an example of this.

8. Is there such a thing as being in a faultfinding mood?

9. Do you think people may criticize the sermons of their pastor? May we ever criticize another person's public prayer? May children criticize their parents?

10. What is wrong with the person who seems to feel he is above criticism?

11. How should we deal with harsh critics? With unfair criticism?

41. Should a Christian Try to Be Popular?
Luke 6:20-38

1. Dale Carnegie wrote *How to Win Friends and Influence People.* Do you think this is also important for a Christian? If we are to be a witness to others, is it not important that they like us?

2. What did Jesus mean when He said, "Woe unto you if all men speak well of you"?

3. Do you think that a "popular" preacher can be more effective in a congregation than an unpopular one?

4. Should we go out of our way to try to be popular, or must this come naturally? What are some of the qualities that make a person popular?

5. It has been proved that when teen-agers in high school like a teacher, they are more liable to study harder in that course and are more likely to choose that subject as the one they take up in college. Do you think a teacher has to be popular to do a good job of teaching?

6. Is it true that if you want others to like you, you must like other people?

7. Why don't people like other people:
   a. who talk a lot but never listen to others?
   b. who have a somber outlook on life?
   c. who are always tense?
   d. who are angry?

8. In high school and college they often have "queens" at the homecoming games. They are usually chosen by a vote of the rest of the students. What kind of girl is usually chosen for this position of honor? On what basis do the students choose them? Is this a good thing?

42. The Rich Fool
Luke 12:13-21

1. This man was prosperous so that he became rich. Is there anything wrong with being rich? Do you think that it is easier for a poor man to be a Christian?

2. This man took good care of his goods. He built larger barns. Was this wrong? Would it not have been better if he had given the surplus away to others?

3. There was a good deal of vanity in this man. What is wrong with vanity? Don't you think a person should be proud of his accomplishments?

4. Somebody calls this man an atheist. Is this a proper way to describe him? What is a practical atheist?

5. This man thought only of this life. Should we forget about this life and think only about the life to come? How can we reach a proper attitude on this matter?

6. He also forgot about the fact that he would have to die. What is the proper attitude toward death? Do you think a Christian should "long to die"? Should we fear death?

7. Do you think the sin of this man was in what he did, or is it something that he neglected to do?

8. Jesus teaches us the proper attitude toward things. Do you think a Christian should be at all interested in earthly things? Is it good to try to become wealthy?

9. A man moved his family to another town in which there was no church of his own denomination because he could get a better job there, with much higher salary. Is this wrong?

10. Should a person give a tenth of all that he makes for the kingdom of God? May he then use the other nine-tenths as he pleases?

11. What does it mean to be "rich toward God"?

43. Putting Away Childish Things
Matthew 11:9-19

1. In this parable Jesus condemns the childish attitudes of the people of His generation. Can you mention some marks of immaturity among people today?

2. Most of us have some childish traits left in us. Is this due to the fact that we have not broken away from our mothers' apron strings?

3. Children will make use of a convenient headache or stomachache to get out of unpleasant work. How does this childish trait still reveal itself in adults?

4. What is wrong with childishness?

5. On T.V. many heroes of Western dramas are presented as real "he-men." Do you think they give a good example of maturity?

6. Some children are described as acting like "little old women" or "little old men." Is this good?

7. Do you think that a person who is emotionally immature can at the same time be spiritually mature?

8. How can we develop greater maturity in ourselves? How can we help our children to be more mature? Is this a process of education or just a matter of better self-control?

9. How can the Christian faith help us to be more mature persons?

10. Jesus' cure for "childishness" is "childlikeness." What is the difference between the two?

44. Four Responses to the Gospel
Matthew 18:1-9, 18-23

1. This parable is often called "The Sower." Would it not be better to call it "The Four Kinds of Hearts"? One writer uses the title "My Audience." Is that right?

2. Why do you think some seed fell by the wayside? Was this wasted seed?

3. What are some of the things that harden the heart so that the seed does not take root?

4. They tell us that an audience absorbs only about one word out of a hundred when a minister preaches. Why is this so?

5. Some people accept the Word with gladness and then soon forget. What makes them do this? Is this a temporary faith, or is there no faith at all?

6. Do you think that it is a good thing to tell a minister, "I enjoyed your sermon"?

7. Some lives are choked with weeds so that they are not fruitful. Jesus mentions some of them.

   a. How does worry prevent people from living fruitful lives?
   b. Why should Jesus mention riches as one of the weeds? Do riches really keep people from accepting the Word?
   c. Jesus also mentions pleasure. Is it wrong for a Christian to enjoy life?
   d. In Luke Jesus also mentions "the lust after things."

8. Notice how Jesus describes the fruitful heart (v. 23). If a person does not understand the Word, is this the fault of the hearer or of the preacher?

9. What are the fruits Jesus desires in our lives?

10. What helps you to listen to a sermon attentively and to live a fruitful life as a result of it? Do you think that preaching really changes the lives of people?

45. Who Is My Neighbor?
Luke 10:30-37

1. Jesus' definition of a neighbor is a bit different from what is evident today. What is the difference in having a neighbor and being a neighbor?

2. Why are some people content to live alone, even when there are people living on both sides of them?

3. Some people are very sympathetic to others in suffering, may even shed a few tears for them, but they never reach out a hand to help. Why?

4. Why are some people more helpful than others to their neighbors? How can you teach your children to be helpful?

5. What does it mean that "compassion must begin at home"?

6. In some countries the old people are taken care of by the family. We put them in nursing homes or homes for the aged. Is this a lack of compassion?

7. Should handicapped children be taken care of by their parents or placed in an institution?

8. Our nation has rather strict exclusion laws in the matter of immigration. We have large sections of the country that are not used, where other nations are vastly overpopulated. Should we change our laws and allow more people to move in?

9. We have vast surpluses of grain and corn. Other countries suffer hunger. Why don't we send some to them?

10. Why do many people feel so reluctant to take help from the benevolent funds of the church, while they have no objection to getting government assistance?

11. Can we be overly sympathetic? Do you think an overly-sympathetic mother makes a good mother? How about an overly-sympathetic nurse?

46. Making Excuses
Luke 14:15-24

1. The men in the parable present excuses for not coming to the feast. Are people today different than they were?

2. Adam blamed his wife for his sin. Married people often blame their mates for their problems. Is this a realistic approach, or is this just making an excuse?

3. Today many people blame heredity or environment for the problems and troubles people have. What do you think of this? Do you think our courts should extend leniency to a person committing a crime because of his early background?

4. Psychiatrists often get their patients to talk about their parents and their early life. Do they do this to find an excuse for the illness of their patients?

5. Many people use the excuse "I'm too busy." What do you think of this? Is this just a "business complex?"

6. Some people will say that they broke down emotionally or mentally because they overworked. Is this true?

7. When people blame the devil for the temptations that come to them, are they giving an explanation or making an excuse?

8. Why do people go to so much trouble to make excuses? Why don't they admit the truth and face up to it?

9. How should we help our children get over this matter of making excuses? Some are very convincing in their excuses. How can you tell whether they are real?

10. One of the defense reactions that is described by psychologists is called "rationalization." This means that a person finds a reasonable explanation for his actions, even though it is not always the whole truth. Why do people use such means? Should it be considered lying, or is it just a part of human weakness?

47. Unprofitable Servants
Luke 17:5-10

1. In this little parable Jesus presents God as a slave owner and man as His slave. Is it ever good for us to look on ourselves as slaves of God?

2. This man represents a hard-hearted slave master. Is God also like that?

3. For some people, work for the kingdom of God seems to be considered more difficult and demanding than the work we do for ourselves and our families. Why is this so?

4. In what way must we describe ourselves as being unprofitable servants?

5. A missionary goes out to a foreign field, requiring much sacrifice. Must this work be described as "unprofitable"?

6. Do we ever perform good works for God?

7. If we are unprofitable servants, why then should we work for God and His kingdom? There is no reward in it—or is there?

8. What is the attitude we should take toward the things we do for God?

9. Would you say that a man like Billy Graham is an unprofitable servant? Or does this only apply to people who do not do much for Christ?

48. Counting the Cost
Luke 14:25-33

1. In these two parables Jesus teaches us that we must count the cost of discipleship. What is the price of discipleship that we should consider?

2. Life is like building a tower. Why do people find it more difficult to make spiritual sacrifices than to make material sacrifices? It is easier to give a few dollars for missions than to give a personal witness. Why?

3. Why does Jesus encourage men to count the cost? Would it not be better to tell of the joys of discipleship than about its cost?

4. Do you feel that many evangelists minimize the cost?

5. Is it true that life is always a battle? Don't you think that for some the road is rather easy?

6. Are people in our country persecuted for their faith in Christ?

7. Don't you feel that people who are always stressing that life is a struggle are also unhappy Christians?

8. Do you think young people have a more difficult battle to fight than older people?

9. How does the song "Onward, Christian Soldiers" apply to the church today?

49. The "Give Me" or the "Make Me" Attitude
Luke 15:11-24

1. In verse 11 the prodigal says, "Give me"; in verse 18 he says, "Make me." This gives insight into this man. What is wrong with the "give me" request?

2. Can you give illustrations of people who take the "give me" attitude today? Do you think it is found among Christians?

3. What makes this young man change his attitude? Does this always work? Are there also selfish Christians?

4. Is it true that all babies are selfish?

5. Is it true that women tend to be less selfish than men? Why?

6. Do you think that people with emotional difficulties have a tendency to think too much in terms of themselves? Is this the cause of the emotional difficulties, or the result?

7. How can we teach our children to be less selfish in their approach to life?

8. Do you think that the shortage of teachers, doctors, nurses, missionaries, etc., is due to the fact that too many people take the "give me" attitude to life?

9. Can a person also be too unselfish for his own good? For example, a person who tries to help other people solve their problems?

10. Satan asks God, "Does Job fear God for naught?" Is it wrong to serve God because of the blessings He gives? Do you think there would be many people who would serve Him if there were no heaven or hell?

11. One writer says, "Do not be so egotistical as to think that you can be purely unselfish." Is this statement true?

50. When Life Becomes Drudgery
Luke 15:25-32

1. There are a number of good things we can say about the elder brother in the parable. For example: he was a worker; he had kept himself clean; he had not run away from home. But Jesus has little good to say for him. Why?

2. The work of the elder brother had become drudgery for him. What makes work drudgery? Is it possible that the same work can be drudgery to one and a joy to another?

3. What are some of the things that rob a person of the joy of work today? Does good pay make work more pleasant? How about the environment in which the work is done?

4. Sometimes a mother with a number of young children finds that the work gets her down, or it "gets under her skin." Why is this so? Does this mean that she does not really love her children or accept them?

5. How can we overcome the spirit of drudgery in our work? Give some practical suggestions.

6. Do you think a person can break down physically or mentally from overwork? Does the attitude with which we do our work make a difference?

7. What was wrong with the attitude of the elder brother toward his father? Toward his borther? Notice that he says, "This, thy son" while the father says, "Thy brother."

8. Do you think the church of today is more ready than the church in the days of Jesus to accept repentant sinners?

9. Why does Jesus present the prodigal son in a more favorable light than the elder brother?

51. The Pitfalls of Pride
Luke 18:9-17

1. The parable presents a picture of a proud man and a humble man at prayer. Someone said about the Pharisee:
   a. He had a good eye for himself.
   b. He had a bad eye for his fellows.
   c. He had no eye on God.

2. Psychologists tell us that a boastful person is really only covering up his own feelings of inferiority and inadequacy. If this is true, is there such a thing as pride?

3. What is the difference between pride and self-esteem?

4. May we say, "I'm proud of my family" or "I'm proud of my house"?

5. Some people might describe a person as being proud, while others might consider the same person to be ambitious, a go-getter or an extrovert. Can we distinguish between these? Does it make a difference as to how we look at a person?

6. Is it possible to have too little pride? Would it be a compliment to say about a person that he has "no pride at all"?

7. Why are proud people hard to live with? What happens when two proud people marry?

8. A sense of pride develops early in life. How can parents help a child develop a sense of pride? What can they do to prevent children from becoming too proud?

9. Why does Jesus condemn the proud man? You notice the same condemnation in the writings of King Solomon and in the Psalms. Why would the Bible refer to this so often?

10. Can a person also become proud of his humility?

11. Should you be proud of your church?

52. A Doubting Prophet—John the Baptist
Matthew 11:1-15

1. John was in prison. He was a brave man for telling Herod about his sin. Don't you think he could have been more diplomatic in his approach? Do you think ministers should tell people to their faces that they are sinners?

2. How could a man who had once said, "Behold the Lamb of God" now ask, "Art thou he that would come, or must we look for another?" Can a true believer have doubts about Christ?

3. Do you think that circumstances in life can lead a person to have spiritual doubts? Was this true of John?

4. There are two kinds of doubt: intellectual and emotional. What kind of doubt did John have?

5. If John doubted that Jesus was the Christ, why did he send his disciples to ask Jesus about it? Is it possible for us to take our doubts to God in prayer?

6. Jesus does not argue with John. Do you think you can ever get rid of doubts by arguments? How do you feel when a person tries to convince you that you have no reason for being depressed? That you should "snap out of it"?

7. In what way was the answer of Jesus the wisest way to deal with the doubts of John? How does this apply to our lives?

8. How do you feel about people who tell you that they never have any doubts in their spiritual life?

9. Should we take our spiritual doubts seriously? Or should we take the attitude that they will pass away?

10. If Christians lived more by faith do you think they would still have emotional and mental illnesses? Does the Christian faith help us to overcome these troubles?

53. Peter—A Vacillating Disciple
Matthew 16:15-23

1. In a brief span of eight verses we hear Peter making a beautiful confession and we hear Jesus calling him a devil. What does this show about the mood swings of this disciple?

2. We all have our ups and downs, but why do some people swing more violently than others? Is this a trait of character with which we are born, or is this something that we have learned?

3. Was the great change that took place in this passage the work of Satan, or did this come from Peter's own vacillating nature?

4. Is it possible to learn to control our moods, or is it merely a matter of learning to live with them? Can we encourage an ugly mood? Can we also fight it?

5. What is the danger of the person who swings into a mood that is above the average level?

6. What is the danger of the person who swings into a mood that is below the average level?

7. How do you react to the person who tells you to treat him kindly because he is in a bad mood? Is it a good thing to tell him to snap out of it?

8. How should we treat our children when they show that they have definite mood swings? Is it possible to help them to conquer this?

9. The man who tends to vacillate spiritually can often have great difficulties in his spiritual life. Note what happened to Peter. How can we learn to live a more consistent spiritual life?

10. God was able to use the impetuous nature of Peter for the welfare of His kingdom. How did He do this?

54. John—A Desire for Greatness
Matthew 20:20-28

1. Jesus chose His disciples from the poorer class of society. John was a fisherman. Why does Jesus' message seem to appeal more to this class? Does it still today?

2. John is called a "son of thunder." He possibly had a hot temper. Does coming to Christ help a person to conquer his temper? Why are there so many angry men today?

3. What do you think of a man who has his mother ask a special favor for him?

4. Don't you think it is a good thing to want to be great in the kingdom of heaven? What was wrong with this request of John?

5. Is it a good thing that a man wants to become an elder or a deacon in the church, or a Sunday school teacher? Should a person ask for this, or should he wait till he is chosen?

6. Why did Jesus deny the request of John's mother?

7. Why was John called "the disciple whom Jesus loved"? Do you feel that a person must be especially lovable to be loved by Christ? Didn't Jesus love all His disciples?

8. What is the relationship between being a disciple and being an apostle?

9. John was a man who showed particular concern for Peter on Easter. What did this indicate about his concern for an erring brother? Why is there so little of this today?

10. Why do we have four Gospel writers? Would it not have been better to have one detailed and consecutive account of the life of Christ?

11. John did achieve greatness when he was given the privilege of writing the Book of Revelation.

55. Making Mountains out of Molehills
Matthew 23:23-28

1. Jesus' strongest words of condemnation were not against the Romans or the social evils of His day, but against the Pharisees and their hypocrisy. Why did He do this?

2. The Pharisees were very concerned about little things, but they neglected the more important things. They had their values mixed up. Does Jesus mean to say that little things are not important?

3. When we say that someone "makes mountains out of molehills," what does this tell about an individual? Why do people get so upset about little things?

4. Do you think it is true that most family quarrels are caused by little things?

5. How can you prevent little annoyances from piling up so that they become big ones and get out of hand?

6. Some people complain a great deal about the little aches and pains in life. What does this show us about such people?

7. Parents will become very angry at a youngster when he spills ink on the rug or breaks a window, but when this same child has an accident and is seriously hurt, they feel that this is in God's providence. How do you explain such inconsistencies?

8. Much of the criticism that is made in life concerns little things, while the more important things are overlooked. What causes this?

9. Do you think that God distinguishes between little things and big things? Are there little sins and big sins?

10. Why is it so important for our mental health to keep from mixing up our mountains and molehills?

11. How does the Christian faith help us to overcome making mountains out of molehills?

56. Touching or Believing
Mark 5:25-34

1. This woman was afflicted with an illness that made her unclean before the Jewish law. She had spent her money on many doctors and had not become well. So now she reaches up and touches the hem of Jesus' robe.

2. She did have faith that Christ could heal her, but was this not more superstition than faith?

3. Do you think people still have this same error?

4. She is not so much interested in Jesus, but she is interested in healing. Do people still have selfish motives in religion?

5. Is it true that many people are more interested in the church and its rites than in Christ Himself?

6. Jesus healed her. Did He reward such imperfect faith? Does Jesus still reward imperfect faith? Is He satisfied with that kind of faith?

7. Why did Jesus make this woman reveal who she was? Was this to show her up, to teach her, or to teach the people that were with Him?

8. This woman said, "I touched thee." Jesus said, "Thy faith hath made thee whole." What is the difference between those two statements?

9. Do you think people are still healed by faith?

10. Does faith have anything to do with our physical condition?

57. Jesus about His Father's Business
Luke 2:41-52

1. The Apocryphal books tell of some of the miracles Jesus performed when He was a boy. What do you think Jesus was like when He was a boy? Don't you think He could have done some miraculous things?

2. When the child Jesus was among the teachers in the temple, does he not seem like a boy who was showing off His knowledge?

3. Mary and Joseph were worried about Jesus. Don't you think that most parents would have worried under similar circumstances? Was it wrong to worry?

4. Mary rebuked Jesus. Was she justified in this? Do you think Jesus ever had to be spanked? If He didn't, was He really a normal child?

5. What was "my Father's business" that Jesus spoke about? Was Jesus fully aware at that time what it was?

6. We must also be about our Father's business. How can we tell what this is for our own lives? Don't we sometimes make mistakes in our choices?

7. Do you feel that ministers and missionaries are more active in the Father's business than farmers, housewives and lawyers? How do you like the term "full-time Christian service"?

8. Why *must* Jesus be about His Father's business? Could He not do as He pleased? What is the *must* that drives the Christian to serve God? Do we "have to" go to church to be saved?

9. How can we tell whether we are active in our Father's business?

10. In view of the answer Jesus gives His parents in verse 49, do you think He treated them with respect?

58. Martha—A Modern Slave
Luke 10:38-42

1. Somebody has said about this family, "If Mary was gone Lazarus would have been lonely, but if Martha was gone he would have been hungry." What do you think?

2. Martha was rather fussy about her work. Is it wrong to be fussy about housework or entertaining?

3. Does a fussy housekeeper make a good wife? Or mother? What kind of atmosphere does this create in the home?

4. Jesus rebukes Martha for worrying too much. Why do people worry? How can you overcome the habit of worrying?

5. Some people have described Mary as a "pious do-nothing," and Martha a practical housekeeper. What do you think? A number of churches have Mary-Martha circles. Is that a good name for a women's organization?

6. Martha is also critical and faultfinding. Is this an indication that she was basically selfish?

7. Do you think wives and mothers are busier today than they were in a previous generation? Why do people complain about being too busy?

8. How do you react to a person who says that he is too busy to go to church, or to read the Bible, or to have time for social activities in the church?

9. Do you think children respect a mother who has become a slave for the family? Do you think husbands appreciate the Martha type of housewife?

10. Don't you think that Martha has rather a sharp tongue to Mary?

11. Jesus said, "But one thing is needful." What is that one thing that is more important than anything else? Where can we find this today?

59. The Art of Giving Thanks
Luke 17:11-19

1. All these men had the same illness and received the same gifts, but only one gave thanks. Do you think the proportion of thankful people is better today?

2. Why do some people complain about the weather, their aches and pains, or conditions in general?

3. Do you think that ingratitude is often due to thoughtlessness? Is this just poor manners? Or is this sinful?

4. Someone said, "I don't owe any man a thing." Is this ever true? Do pride and gratitude ever go together?

5. Should you ever thank someone when you don't really mean it? Should you tip a waitress even though you have received poor service?

6. Do you think there is more gratitude among the wealthy than among the poor? Among the healthy than among the sick?

7. Do you think a loving God would send us illness to teach us to appreciate our health more?

8. Should we ever take things for granted? Are there not some things that we must take for granted to live successfully in this world?

9. When Mother prepares a meal and the family gives no word of appreciation, she may feel badly about this. Is Mother wrong, or the family?

10. How can we teach our children to be more thankful—and to express it more?

11. Is it good to compare our own circumstances with those of others? What is usually the result?

12. Whom would you prefer as a mate in life: one who sends flowers and gifts, but who does not express appreciation in words; or one who expresses his gratitude and love in words, but sends no flowers or gifts?

60. Zacchaeus—The Publican
Luke 19:1-10

1. Zacchaeus was short of stature. What are some of the disadvantages of this? Do you think that short people tend to overreact because of their handicap?

2. Why would a man choose to be a tax-collector in those days?

3. The Jewish people despised the publicans and would not let their children marry a son or daughter of one of them. Were they justified in taking this attitude? Is this not an extreme case of intolerance?

4. What are some of the dangers of being rich? Do you think it is more difficult for a rich man to be saved than for a poor man?

5. Why did Jesus take a special interest in publicans? Matthew, a publican, was one of His disciples, and Jesus often visited with his friends.

6. Was Zacchaeus only curious to see Jesus, or do you think there was a desire to find salvation?

7. Zacchaeus was converted to faith in Christ. Do you think there is advantage in having a definite conversion experience? What are some of the dangers of being a Christian from childhood on? Do all people need to be converted?

8. When Zacchaeus was converted he told Jesus he was going to pay back what he had taken by cheating the people. Is it necessary to make restitution if we are to find forgiveness? Is this doing penance for the wrongs we have done?

9. Why was it easier for a publican than for a Pharisee to be led to salvation? Is this still true?

61. Peter—On Satan's Sieve
Luke 22:31-34, 54-62

1. Jesus warns Peter in a special way at a time when he had a lot of self-confidence. Is there also a healthy self-confidence?

2. Why must Satan ask God for permission to sift Peter as wheat? Is this also true for our temptations?

3. Why does God allow Peter to be sifted?

4. Peter was a man of violent mood swings. How did Satan get at Peter in the night of the trial?

5. The sifting process was used to separate the wheat and the chaff. How are we being sifted today?

6. Peter denied his Lord three times. This is a rather common sin. Why did it bother Peter so much? Do you feel that we are sufficiently concerned about it today?

7. The denial of Peter was used to make a better man out of him. How can a sinful act be helpful in a person's life?

8. What kept Peter from falling through Satan's sieve?

9. What does this account show us about the role of Satan in the life of a Christian? How about the relationship of Christ to Satan?

10. Peter went out and wept. Why does it seem more difficult for a man than for a woman to weep?

62. Judas—The Traitor
Luke 22:1-6, 47-53

1. Why was Judas chosen by Jesus, and why did Judas choose to follow Jesus and become one of the Twelve?

2. Why did he turn against Jesus in the way and at the time that he did?

3. Do you think the other disciples suspected that Judas was not honest and that he would betray Jesus?

4. At Bethany Judas made the remark, "Why was not this ointment sold and [the money] given to the poor?" Was this not a rather pious statement on his part?

5. What does it mean that "Satan entered into the heart of Judas"? Was he possessed of a demon? Was this just a temptation? Could Judas help himself when Satan entered his heart?

6. Do you think that Judas was really interested in the thirty pieces of silver, or was this really a hatred for the Christ?

7. In the upper room Jesus practically points out Judas to the rest of the disciples when they all ask, "Is it I?" Why did Jesus do this? Why did the disciples find it so hard to accept this?

8. What does it mean that Judas betrayed Jesus with a kiss? Why is this considered to be so terrible?

9. Peter also committed a great sin in the same night. It was not so different from that of Judas. Why was the sin of Judas so much worse than that of Peter? Why were the results so different?

10. Did Judas still have a conscience? How did he show this?

11. Could Judas have repented from this sin after he had committed it?

12. Are we ever guilty of the sin of Judas in our relationship with Jesus? Or our relationship with each other?

63. The Journey to Emmaus
Luke 24:13-32

1. These two men knew about Good Friday but not about Easter. Why should this make them feel so hopeless? Do you think this accounts for the gloomy outlook of many today?

2. Jesus opened the Scriptures to Cleopas and his friend. Why is the Bible a closed book to many people today? How can it become an open book?

3. Do you feel that there are many people in the church who know about Christ, but who do not know Him? What is the difference? Is it possible that our emphasis on creeds and doctrines prevents people from really knowing Christ personally?

4. These men spoke of having "burning hearts." Isn't this a rather emotional approach to faith in Christ? Is there a danger of too much emotionalism in the church? What is wrong with emotionalism?

5. John Calvin's crest included the symbol of a burning heart held in an outstretched palm. Do you think this is a good motto also for the church today? How can we develop more of this warmth of spiritual life?

6. Do you feel that our worship service should include more factors that would stir the emotions, such as livelier hymns, more emotional preaching and an altar call?

7. Should the emphasis of the church be to instruct people, or to stir people to greater devotion for Christ?

8. Do you feel that there is as much warmth in the hearts of believers in a time of affluence as there would be in a time of stress or poverty?

9. Pierre Berton speaks of the *Lukewarm Pulpit* and the *Comfortable Pew*. Do you feel that his criticism of the church is justified; What can be done to remedy the situation?

64. The Woman at Jacob's Well

John 4:1-14

1. The Jews and the Samaritans did not like each other. Was there a good reason for this? Was this just an example of Jewish intolerance?

2. Don't you find it rather hard to understand how Jesus, the Son of God, could become thirsty and tired? What does it tell us about the Christ?

3. The woman at the well was evidently not a person with a good reputation, especially in her relationship with men. Wasn't it a bit indiscreet for Jesus to be there with her alone? Today people would not consider it proper if a minister would do this. Why not?

4. Jesus makes use of good evangelistic methods with this woman. Notice that He first becomes acquainted with her and then leads her to spiritual matters. Is it important to use good methods of evangelism, or will the gospel message take care of itself when we present it?

5. The central core of evangelism is a personal confrontation with the Christ. How does Jesus lead her to this point? Do you feel that this is stressed enough in modern evangelism and preaching?

6. What does it mean to worship in spirit and in truth? Does this imply that we can just as well worship God when we are alone with Him in nature as when we are in church?

7. Does the form of worship that is used in our churches help to worship in spirit and in truth? How could it be improved?

8. What is the living water of which Jesus speaks in verse 14?

9. Was this woman at Jacob's well genuinely converted?

65. Attitudes toward Sinners
John 8:1-11

1. The Pharisees brought to Jesus a woman taken in the act of adultery. Why didn't they bring her partner in sin? Is it true that a woman should set the standards in such matters?

2. The Pharisees took a condemnatory attitude. What is wrong with this approach? Do you think people still have this attitude?

3. Why does Jesus defend a woman who was obviously guilty of a sin? Does He not take sin seriously?

4. What did Jesus write in the sand?

5. These men were convicted in their consciences by what Jesus wrote. What is the reason for having a guilty conscience? Some things may bother your conscience and they will not bother someone else's. Why the difference?

6. Jesus does not condemn the sinner. Does He condemn her sin?

7. May we ever condemn another person for a sin he has committed? May we criticize him?

8. Should parents condemn their children for sins they commit? What should our attitude be if, for example, a child steals something? Or if a daughter is guilty of adultery?

9. Can parents be too lenient in dealing with children who commit some obvious sin?

10. Can parents be too severe with children who do things that are wrong?

11. Jesus speaks about the need of forgiveness. Is it true that we must learn to forgive others if we want to enjoy forgiveness ourselves?

12. Why is it important to learn to forgive ourselves, if we have committed some sin?

66. Why?
John 9:1-5; Judges 6:13; Job 3:2-26

1. What was wrong with the question asked by the disciples in John 9:1? Does the answer of Jesus imply that there is no relationship between sin and sickness?

2. Gideon asked the question "why" in a cynical way. What do you think of that attitude?

3. Job asks, "Why does God give life to a person when it leads to so much suffering?" Is this a healthy attitude to take?

4. In God's answer to Gideon's question, He tells Gideon to get to work and do something about it. How can this help to answer our *why's?* Do you feel that many people who are suffering today could use this advice?

5. What makes people ask this question? Is it just curiosity or is it a genuine concern to find the answer?

6. Is it a good thing to look back into our past and try to discover why we react the way we do today?

7. What do you think of the person who says, "Why did this happen to me, of all people. I have done so much good in my life. I have served the Lord all my days. Why should God deal with me now in this harsh way?"

8. How do you feel when a person tells you that it is a sin to ask the question, "why?"

9. What answer to the Christian's question do we find in the words of Jesus, "Why hast thou forsaken me?"

10. What is more important in sickness—to look back or to look ahead? Should a person say, "Why has all this befallen me," or "To what end is God using this suffering?"

67. Jesus Washing the Disciples' Feet
John 13:1-15

1. Jesus takes the place of the slave among His disciples. Don't you think Jesus lost some of His dignity when He did this? Why is it hard for us to think of the Son of God in the form of a slave?

2. How do you like Peter's reaction to this ceremony?

3. Some churches still use the ceremony of foot-washing. Do you think it would be beneficial to have this ceremony in our churches today?

4. In this ceremony Jesus was not thinking so much of our cleansing from sin through regeneration, but rather the daily cleansing from sin. Do we have sins every day that need to be forgiven? What do you think of those who say they are perfect—the perfectionists?

5. The disciples had been arguing about who was the greatest among them. Isn't it a good thing to seek for an important position in the church or in the kingdom? What was wrong with the spirit of the disciples?

6. Jesus tries to teach His disciples to be humble. Why is it so hard to learn humility? Do you think that some people are naturally more humble than others? Are children naturally humble or must they learn this?

7. How does the ceremony of foot-washing teach us to be more humble?

8. Do you think a person can be too humble?

9. Jesus teaches us that we are to help our fellow-men, even when it means that we must stoop to serve. Why is there so much "non-involvement" with others today? Can a person also become too involved?

68. Caiaphas—The Formalist
John 11:45-54

1. Caiaphas was High Priest that year. He wore the robes of a priest, but it was only outward show. Why would a person be interested in only a formal religion?

2. Is there a danger that our worship becomes too formal? Some churches have informal worship services. How would you react to them in your church?

3. A person can pray while lying in bed. Is there any advantage to kneeling for prayer? Would it be well to kneel in our church services?

4. Is there a danger of laying too much emphasis on the church so that people fall into the error of "churchiness"? Why are you a member of your particular church?

5. What is the difference between confessing our faith and "joining church"?

6. There is a lot of formalism in our social life. Is it proper to say, "How nice to see you" when you really do not mean it? Should a person be really honest about the sermon when he shakes hands with the minister after the service?

7. John indicates that Caiaphas meant the statement he made for evil, but that God uses this wicked statement as a prophecy. Does this mean that God uses a sinful act for good? Do our sinful acts also work out for the good?

8. Should we present ourselves to others just as we are, or is it permissible to show our best side? Is this being dishonest?

9. How can we overcome the sin of formalism in our own lives and in those of our children?

69. Pilate—The Coward
John 19:1-11

1. Pilate happened to be the representative of the Roman Empire to sit in judgment over Jesus. His name goes down in history as that of an unjust judge. John tells us that he was afraid. Of whom was he afraid?

2. Why do you think Pilate was so afraid at this time?

3. Do you think an unbeliever like Pilate is more inclined to be filled with fear than a believer? Why?

4. How does Pilate handle his fears?

5. Pilate's fears became worse when he heard of the dream of his wife. Do you think our dreams give information that we do not have when we are awake?

6. Pilate washes his hands and says, "I am innocent." Do you think that this quieted his conscience?

7. In what way do some people try to quiet their conscience today much as Pilate did on Good Friday?

8. How must we quiet our consciences?

9. God had determined that Jesus would die. Does this mean that Pilate was not fully to blame for this crime? How do we explain this?

10. In verse 22 Pilate says, "What I have written, I have written." In what way was this true for Pilate? Is this also true for us?

11. When Jesus prayed, "Father, forgive them," did this also include Pilate? Did God forgive him?

70. Joseph—A Secret Disciple
John 19:38-42

1. We read of Joseph of Arimathea only a few times in the New Testament. We are told that he was wealthy, that he was a "good and upright man" and that he was a member of the Jewish Council.

2. Do you think that having wealth made it harder for Joseph to be a disciple of Jesus?

3. The position of honor that Joseph held would make it hard for him to confess Christ. Why?

4. How could a "good and upright" man be a member of the Jewish Sanhedrin?

5. Can a person be a true Christian and yet be a secret follower of Jesus?

6. Do you think a person can be a secret follower of Christ for a long period of time, or would this soon become evident?

7. What is wrong with hiding our convictions? Should we always tell people just what we believe, or are there times when we should minimize our differences?

8. Joseph allowed Jesus to use his grave. What did this show as to the estimate that he had of Jesus?

9. Joseph reveals his faith in Christ at the time of Jesus' crucifixion. How did this help him to develop the courage of his convictions?

10. How can we develop more courage to confess Christ before men? Is this something that can also be overdone?

71. Thomas—Faith without Sight
John 20:24-31

1. Thomas is often called a doubter, but possibly it is better to describe him as a pessimist. What is wrong with a Christian who has a tendency to look at the gloomy side of life?

2. If a person has a gloomy disposition, can anything be done to change this?

3. Thomas stayed away from the meeting of the disciples. Is this something like a depressed person who feels uneasy in church? Is it permissible to stay away from the worship services when you feel this way?

4. Was it wrong for Thomas to ask for visible signs and tangible proofs? Is it easier to believe when we can touch and see the object of faith, such as, some direct answer to prayer?

5. Why is it more blessed to believe without seeing?

6. What brought Thomas to the wonderful confession that he makes in verse 28? Do you think Jesus used good psychology and therapy on Thomas?

7. Do you think it is good to have some doubts intermingled with our faith? What good purpose could they have?

8. How can we overcome our spiritual doubts? Is this only a matter of our trust in God, or does this also involve our mental and emotional stability?

9. The only sign Jesus gave to Thomas was that of His nail-pierced hands and His wounded side.

72. Peter—Overly Concerned about Tomorrow
John 21:18-23

1. Jesus spoke about Peter's future. It seems a bit strange that Peter does not refer to his own death, even though it is interpreted to refer to martyrdom. Is this a normal Christian reaction to such a prediction?

2. Why was it wrong for Peter to ask about John's future?

3. Should a Christian make plans for the future? Solomon says that a man who does not plan for the future is a fool.

4. Someone estimated that 60 percent of our worries are about the future, 30 percent about the past and 10 percent about the present. What do you think?

5. What does it mean to leave the future in God's hand; How can a person do this?

6. Do you think it is wrong to try to gain knowledge of the future by means of fortune tellers or horoscopes?

7. Should a doctor tell a person who has an incurable illness that he has only six months to live?

8. If we knew there was to be some serious illness in our family or some great sorrow in our life within six months, what would it do to our life?

9. Jesus tells Peter not to sit idly staring into the future but "Follow thou me." How can such a command rid us of an over-concern about the future?

10. There are many Christians who expect that Christ will return soon. How do you feel about this? How does it affect our lives?

73. Barnabas—The Portrait of a Good Man
Acts 4:31-37; 11:19-24

1. His real name was Joseph, but he was given the name Barnabas, "Son of Consolation." He had the ability to console and cheer people. What qualities of character does this name suggest? Do you think that pastors should console people, or is it better that they have the ability to stir people up a bit?

2. He was a wealthy man. Why is it unusual for a rich man to become a missionary?

3. His goodness becomes evident when he sells his farm and gives the money to the church. Is liberal giving always the mark of a good man?

4. Do you blame Peter and John for not accepting Paul the persecutor when he came to Jerusalem? Did Barnabas take a risk when he took Paul in and introduced him to the disciples at Jerusalem?

5. Usually Barnabas lived in the shadow of Paul. Why do many people find it so hard to take second place?

6. Paul and Barnabas were both good men, and yet they had a serious quarrel. Can good men also quarrel? Who was right, Paul or Barnabas in the dispute about John Mark? Was Barnabas too goodhearted?

7. In Acts 11:24 we are given the secret of what it means to be a good man. "He was full of the Holy Spirit and of faith." What is the difference between having the Holy Spirit and being full of the Holy Spirit? Is a person ever perfectly filled with the Spirit?

8. How does faith enter into this picture? Does every one who has faith in Christ also have the Holy Spirit in him? How are faith and the indwelling Spirit related?

74. I Found Christ on the Highway
Acts 8:26-40

1. This man was important in the government of Ethiopia. Usually people in high places are not noted for a deep interest in religion. Is there reason for this?

2. Philip was directed by the Spirit to go to meet him. Does God still direct His ministers in this way? Do you think the Holy Spirit guides ministers when they decide on a call from another church?

3. Why could not this man find a satisfying answer to his spiritual problems in Jerusalem?

4. Philip talked with this man and led him to his conversion. Do you think that people who have a special conversion experience can be more sure of their salvation than those who have lived in the church all their lives?

5. Don't you think Philip was a little hasty when he baptized this man and took him into the church? Today we insist that someone who wants to enter the church must first be instructed in the doctrines of the church.

6. This was evidently the first Negro convert that came into the church. Is it good to bring people of various races together in the same church?

7. This man went on his way rejoicing. Why are there so many Christians today who do not have much Christian joy in their lives?

8. This story shows the working of God's providence in a remarkable way. Is the providence of God still active in the world? If God has provided for all things, why then should we still work? Why should we pray?

75. Jesus Appeals to Paul
Acts 9:1-9

1. Why would a man like Paul spend all his time persecuting the Christians? Would you describe him as an "angry man"?

2. Do you think people are more tolerant toward Christians today? Why would this be so? Is this good or bad?

3. Was the light that shone from heaven a natural thing, or was it a miracle?

4. Do you think Paul really heard the voice of the Lord? Does God still speak to people in this direct way? How does He speak to us?

5. Why did Jesus say, "Why persecutest thou *me*"? Why did He not say, "Why do you persecute my *church*"? What does this question show us about the way Jesus identifies Himself with His suffering children?

6. Paul was suddenly converted. Do you think all people need this kind of conversion?

7. In verse 5 Jesus tells Paul he has been kicking against the goad. This would indicate that Paul had been fighting back against the call of Christ. In what way do people resist the call of God?

8. Why did God choose a man like Paul to become the great missionary? Could He not have chosen someone who had a better record?

9. What character traits of Paul made him a great missionary?

76. Paul in Damascus
Acts 9:10-20

1. Saul the Persecutor became Paul the Apostle. It took an act of God to change him. Actually it took fourteen years before he was ready to go out as a missionary. This presents one of the steps on the road to apostleship.

2. God spoke to Ananias, but he was reluctant to go. Why was Ananias so afraid? Was his fear justified? Was this a good excuse for disobeying God's orders?

3. Why is it so difficult to witness to a person who is opposed to Christ?

4. God said, "Behold he prayeth." Had Paul never prayed before? What is the difference between saying our prayers and praying?

5. How did Paul learn to pray in those few days? How must we learn to pray?

6. People often pray when they are in trouble, but not so much when they prosper. What is wrong in this? Is it true that if we do not pray when we are prosperous we will also not be able to truly pray in time of trouble?

7. Ananias laid his hands on Paul and he was healed of his blindness. Was this miraculous healing? Was Ananias a faith healer like Oral Roberts? Do you believe in faith healing?

8. Paul was baptized by Ananias a few minutes after he made his confession. Was this not a bit sudden? Why do we make people learn the catechism or attend a confession class? Would it not be better to take people into the church first and then instruct them?

9. Ananias heard the voice of God speaking to him. If we stated that God spoke to us people would say we are mentally sick. What is the difference?

10. Don't you think it was a little foolish for Paul to start preaching at Damascus when he knew he would be persecuted for it?

77. Peter—A Lesson in Tolerance
Acts 10:9-16

1. Peter was the leader of the group in the early church who felt that a Gentile must first accept the Jewish faith and then become a Christian. God teaches him a lesson by means of this vision.

2. "What God has cleansed, call thou not common or unclean." Does this mean that we may never call anyone unclean? Must we accept all people—even those living in great sin?

3. How do you explain that there is so much intolerance in an enlightened nation such as ours?

4. Is it also possible to be too tolerant?

5. How far should we go with segregation or desegregation in our country? Should we take people of various races into the same church, or would it be better to help them set up their own churches?

6. If a man has his own barber shop, or motel, is it not his constitutional right to select his customers? Should he be forced to take anyone who comes along?

7. Why is it so difficult to do mission work among the Jews? Why has the Jew been hated by others throughout history?

8. How does the Christian faith help us overcome the spirit of intolerance?

9. Do some church groups tend to be more tolerant than other church groups? What are some reasons for this?

10. How do people show intolerance in everyday life?

11. What is the answer to intolerance that is given to Peter in this passage? How does this still apply?

78. An Unexpected Answer to Prayer
Acts 12:6-17

1. Peter was in prison, guarded by sixteen soldiers. Herod intended to execute him in the morning. Why was Peter able to sleep soundly during that night? Do you think you could sleep soundly under similar circumstances?

2. The church had an all-night prayer session. What do you think of such long sessions of prayer? Don't they lead to a lot of vain repetition?

3. Does God answer united prayer more readily than the prayer of an individual? Some people will say when they recovered from a serious operation, "A lot of people were praying for me." Does this help?

4. When the church at Jerusalem prayed they did not really expect that God was going to answer their prayer. What is wrong with this kind of prayer? Or were they just being realistic about the matter?

5. Is there always a measure of doubt intermingled with our prayers?

6. If God has all things controlled by His providence, what is the value of prayer? Does prayer really change things?

7. When our nation is at war is it proper to pray for victory? How do we know that God is on our side?

8. When we pray for something must we really believe that God is going to give us what we ask for? If we ask that God's will may be done, does this not detract from the power of our prayer?

9. Are there unanswered prayers?

10. Billy Graham often mentions that he feels that the success of his campaigns is due to the prayers sent up in behalf of this work. How could we apply this to the ministry of the average church? Is it possible that the lack of growth of the Christian church is due to a lack of fervent prayer?

79. When Christians Disagree
Acts 15:35-41

1. There was considerable controversy in the early church. In verse 2—"There was no small dissension" and in verse 39—"There was sharp contention." Why was there so much disagreement at that time? Why is there so much today?

2. When two people cannot reach an agreement, is it a good policy to agree to disagree? Does this also present a solution in family problems?

3. Is it a good thing that Christians disagree?

4. Someone says that most disagreements come about because people are stubborn. Is this true?

5. Is it possible for a person to be too agreeable with others?

6. What is wrong with the kind of person who can see only one side of a subject? Is this being narrow-minded? Should a Christian be broad-minded?

7. Is there too much controversy in the church and among denominations? Don't you think it would be better if denominations would unite and make one large church?

8. When two Christians have a disagreement, how should they go about solving their dispute?

9. How must husbands and wives solve their disagreements?

10. How must parents solve disagreements with their children? Should they ever compromise?

11. The dispute between Paul and Barnabas worked out for the best interests of the church, since two teams set out on missionary journeys, instead of one. Do you think that disagreements often work out to some real advantage?

80. Lydia—A Christian Business Woman
Acts 16:9-16

1. Lydia was a business woman. She evidently had a family. What do you think about mothers who work outside of the home? What are some of the dangers? Why do mothers work?

2. Lydia worshiped God with a few others at the riverside. Do you think we spend too much money on church buildings that are used only a few hours a week? Do you feel that the money spent on great cathedrals is wasted?

3. Lydia heard the Word that was preached. This is commonly considered to the the external call of God. Does everyone who goes to church "hear the Word"?

4. "The Lord opened her heart." How does this take place? How do we know that the Lord has opened our heart? Do we have anything to do with this ourselves, or is this all the work of God?

5. Don't you think the baptism of Lydia was rather hasty? Would it not have been better for her to have had instruction for a few weeks, or months? Why don't we baptize people immediately?

6. From now on the church meets at the home of Lydia. Today there is much emphasis on small group meetings within the church, such as Bible study and prayer groups. What is the advantage of such group meetings? What are the dangers connected with small groups within the church?

7. Do you think people are as hospitable today as they were some years ago? Why are people reluctant to invite guests to stay in their home?

8. The church at Philippi was one that Paul seemed to love very much. Why would Paul have a particular interest in this church?

81. Our Three Judges
I Corinthians 4:3, 4

1. "In every man there are four men:" as the world sees him, as his loved ones see him, as he sees himself, and as God sees him.

2. May we be indifferent to public opinion? Should we be a slave to it? Should a Christian try to be popular?

3. Are our friends and loved ones more critical of us than strangers are? Why? Is it good if a husband can see no faults in his wife, or a wife none in her husband?

4. Do you think that any of us have an unbiased opinion of ourselves? What is wrong with a person who thinks too little of himself?

5. What is the danger of thinking too much of ourselves? It is often said that people who carry an air of superiority are only covering up inferiority feelings. Is this true?

6. What is wrong with human judgments on any level—either that of our enemies, our friends, or ourselves? Can one person really judge another person?

7. "He that judgeth me is the Lord." Notice that it does not say, "Shall judge." How do we know what God's judgment is of us?

8. If a person looks at life through the eyes of a depression he feels that he is no good and that God also feels that way about him. How can we overcome that feeling?

9. Schools make a good deal of use of psychological tests. Do they give a true evaluation of our children? What value do they have? What are their dangers?

10. How can a person gain a true estimation of himself?

82. Christian Liberty
I Corinthians 8:8-13

1. Some things are directly commanded by God in the Bible; other things are directly forbidden. But there is also an area of conduct in which we may choose. This is the part of life that concerns our Christian liberty.

2. Some people consider all things to be either good or bad; they see only blacks and whites but no greys. What makes people react this way to life? What are the dangers of such attitudes?

3. How must we react to others who differ from us in such matters as smoking or what may properly be done on the Lord's day? Do others have a right to impose their will on us?

4. Things that seem to be wrong to some people do not seem to be wrong to others. Why is there this difference among Christians?

5. Do you think Christians can be too strict in their Christian life?

6. Is it a good thing for parents to enforce their view of what is right and wrong on their children? Would it not be better to let them do their own choosing?

7. Our Christian liberty is limited when we become a stumbling block to others. When does something become a stumbling block or offense to others?

8. Do you think a Christian can be a professional baseball player? A professional boxer? A successful entertainer?

9. Some churches have laid down certain rules by which they expect their members to live. Is this the right thing to do, or should the church honor the Christian liberty of its members?

10. Do you think something could be wrong for one person and be permissible for another (e.g., having a cocktail before dinner)?

83. Getting Along with Other People
I Corinthians 9:19-27

1. In verse 22 Paul tells us that he had become "all things to all men." Why is this statement sometimes used as a criticism of certain ministers?

2. When does sticking to our convictions become just plain stubbornness?

3. Some people are very rigid in their way of thinking. They see only one side of every question. Why do you think people are that way?

4. Is it good to try to be popular?

5. Some people are described as being "narrow-minded." Is this good or bad? Teen-agers will sometimes consider their parents to be narrow-minded because they cannot agree with them on certain issues.

6. In the church we sometimes call people who are not of the same faith "outsiders." What do you think of that?

7. Is it possible for a person to be too agreeable with others? Where do we find the happy medium?

8. How do you like a book like Dale Carnegie's *How to Win Friends and Influence People?*

9. What is Paul's basis for being "all things to all men"?

10. What should be our attitude toward people of other races? Of other religions?

11. In the movement toward church union (the ecumenical movement) much emphasis is laid on trying to find common grounds of agreement and overlooking some of the differences. Do you feel that a good union of churches can be established on this basis? Can you suggest something better?

84. The Captivity of Our Thoughts
II Corinthians 10:5

1. Our thoughts are a most marvelous gift of a bountiful Creator. They are part of the image of God in man. What has been the result of sin on the human mind?

2. Is it true that sin always begins in the mind? Is there also thoughtless sin?

3. Is it just as wrong to think something evil as to do something evil? Matthew 5:21-28.

4. How does the saving work of Christ affect our thoughts?

5. Paul gives a good suggestion as to how to achieve captivity of thought in the first part of I Corinthians 10:5. How can we do this?

6. Is it possible to control our thinking? How must it be done?

7. Paul gives a list of things in Philippians 4:8 and then says, "Think on these things." This presents thought control with a positive emphasis. Is this the same as "positive thinking"?

8. How can the Christian faith help us to control depressive thoughts? morose thoughts? evil thoughts? hostile thoughts?

9. Do we ever reach the point where "every thought" is brought into captivity of Christ? Is this just an ideal we strive for, or is this a program for living?

10. Do you think the influence of T.V. and modern magazines is a good one on the minds of children? On our own minds?

11. How can you control your thoughts while in church? While you are praying?

85. Are There Unanswered Prayers?
II Corinthians 12:6-10; Deuteronomy 3:23-29

1. Some people say it is wrong to speak about unanswered prayer. What do people commonly mean when they use this term?

2. In I Peter 3:7 Peter speaks about "hindered" prayer. What kinds of things can hinder our prayers?

3. When God says to Moses, "Speak no more to me concerning this matter" does God limit his prayer? Are there any limits to prayer today? Should we keep on praying that God will make a mentally handicapped child normal again?

4. When we think that our prayers are not answered, what should we do? How can we determine that our prayers are not answered?

5. In the story *Three Men on a Raft* Capt. Eddie Rickenbaker and the other two men that were with him prayed for help. God sent rain and also a sea gull landed on the raft. He then writes, "Now I know that God answers prayer." What do you think of that kind of reasoning?

6. Does prayer change the plan of God? If God has all things planned anyway, what is the use of praying?

7. What do you think of the statement, "I believe in prayer"?

8. During World War II a mother went every day to church to pray for her son's safety. When a notice came from the war department that her son had been killed in action she said, "I'm through with praying. Either there is no God, or He does not care." What was wrong with this attitude?

86. The Proper Use of Time
Ephesians 5:13-21

1. Time is a priceless gift; we can use it only once, and we should use it well. Why does time seem to go by so fast when we enjoy ourselves, and so slowly when we are bored?

2. Do you think it is good to work according to a schedule? What are the dangers?

3. Do you think people are busier today than they were a generation ago? Why?

4. What do you think of the statement "time heals all things"?

5. We often are told to live by the day. But Solomon tells us that if we do not make plans for the future, we are foolish. In what way are we supposed to live by the day?

6. Would it be good for us to know what lies ahead of us for the next year? Why?

7. Do you think people have too much leisure time today?

8. Is it sinful to waste a few minutes or a few hours of our time?

9. A man will say, "I lost two months of my life; I was sick and spent part of that time in a hospital." Is this really lost time?

10. What is wrong with people who are always a bit late? Is punctuality a trait of character, or just a good habit that we develop?

11. What can we do to teach our children to use their time to the best advantage?

12. Is time spent in recreation or play wasted time?

87. Adjustments in Marriage
Ephesians 5:22-33

1. What is wrong with the marriage in which husband and wife are always in perfect agreement?

2. It is often stated that the wife is taking a more dominant role in the family, and that the husband is taking a less dominant role. Do you think this is a good thing? If so, should a bride still promise in the marriage form to "obey" her husband?

3. Why is it not good for a young man to marry a girl "just like the girl that married dear old dad"?

4. Why do some people find it difficult to make adjustments in family living?

5. How can parents help their children to become prepared for marriage? How can parents be a hindrance to the marital adjustments that must be made by their children?

6. We should adjust to our mate in marriage. It is also possible that we should try to change some of the habits and attitudes of our mates. How should we go about this?

7. There are often differences in spiritual attitudes between husband and wife, since each comes from a different family background. There are often different ideas as to what may or may not be done on Sunday. How should we handle these differences? May we ever compromise just to have peace in the family?

8. If there are differences between husband and wife that cannot be resolved, would you call in a third party to help solve the problem?

9. Do you feel that a marriage has a better chance of succeeding if there is premarital counseling? Who should do this kind of counseling?

10. Do you feel that the Christian faith solves all marriage problems? Does it help?

88. Don't Blame Your Parents
Ephesians 6:1-9

1. "If you want to have good mental health be sure to choose your parents wisely." Do you think this is true? Is environment more important than hereditary?

2. "You do not inherit a sickness, but only a disposition towards an illness, either emotional or physical." What do you think of this statement?

3. What are some of the things we have by means of heredity, and what are the things we gain by our environment?

4. Do we inherit only from our parents, or also our grandparents and great-grandparents? How far back does this go?

5. A young fellow said, "It's no wonder that I have a hot temper because my dad also had one." Does this make a good excuse?

6. Abraham Lincoln came from a poor family background, but he became President of the United States. Some criminals come from very good homes. How can we explain this?

7. Does heredity, or environment, lessen our own personal responsibility?

8. Why does a psychiatrist try to get a person to talk about his early life and his family background? Is this done to blame the parents for mental and emotional troubles?

9. Each of us is a link in the chain of the generations. Mention some implications of this fact.

10. Judges and courts are often especially lenient with offenders who come from a broken home, or when their parents are irresponsible. Is this good or bad? Do you think God also takes this into account when He judges us?

89. The Strengthening of the Will
Romans 7:14-25; Philippians 2:12-15

1. The will is a fundamental power in our lives. It is hard to define. It is that power that inspires us to think, to act, to respond—in fact, any of the abilities we have. It is behind all we do.

2. When we describe someone as having a "weak will," what do we mean? How does it show itself?

3. Napoleon is described as a man of tremendous will power. How did he show this? Was it good or bad?

4. Is it possible for a good man to have a weak will?

5. To develop a Christian will power there must also be a conversion of the will. How was this evident in the life of Paul?

6. How can a person strengthen his will?

7. Do you think our childhood training tends to influence us as far as having a weak or a strong will? How can parents help their youngsters develop will power?

8. Well-meaning people often tell patients to "snap out" of their difficulties, or they say, "If you only used your will power more." What do you think of such advice?

9. Do you think that the "will to live" or the "will to get better" are important in recovering from any sickness?

10. A man facing a difficult task says, "I will do it" but he adds, "I don't think I can." What does this show about his will? Do you think this is a good way to face such a task?

11. Someone has said that to develop will power we need to add a third dimension. What is that third dimension?

12. How can we develop the will power to keep on a diet or break a bad habit?

13. What part does will power play in building a new habit?

90. The Art of Forgetting
Philippians 3:10-16

1. Paul tells us to forget the things that are behind. This implies that we are to learn the art of forgetting. Can a person really forget his past mistakes?

2. Someone says, "Tell me what you remember best and I will tell you what kind of a man you are." What do you think of this statement?

3. Sometimes past events will have been forgotten for a long time, and yet when we become ill they come back to our minds so clearly. Why?

4. How can we learn to forget that someone has hurt us in one way or another?

5. Should we also learn to forget past successes?

6. By her actions a daughter had seriously hurt the feelings of her mother. The mother said, "I will forgive, but I can never forget." What do you think of this statement?

7. Why must we learn to forget about the past, according to Paul in verses 13 and 14?

8. How can we learn to forget the ugly things that have happened in our past?

9. Why does a psychiatrist try to make us remember the things that happened to us, sometimes even in our childhood? Wouldn't it be better to forget these things?

10. Someone has said, "You will remember the things you want to remember, and you will forget the things you want to forget." Do you think this is true?

11. Does God forget our sins?

91. The Secret of Contentment
Philippians 4:1-11

1. Contentment means to be restful and quiet of mind in our present condition. It is a lack of discontent not to murmur or complain.

2. Does contentment mean that a man has a spirit of indifference—that he does not care what happens to him? Does it mean that a man is satisfied with himself?

3. A person says, "I am resigned to my fate." Is this a good attitude?

4. Must a person be satisfied with whatever he has, or should he strive to improve himself?

5. Paul says that he had learned to be content. How does a person learn this? Is this not something that we have from our youth?

6. Why do you think there is so little real contentment today?

7. Paul was in prison when he wrote this. Is it a good thing when a person is content to be in a hospital?

8. Is it true that people who are wealthy and healthy are more content than people who are sick or poor?

9. Do you think there is any person who is really content with things as they are?

10. Somebody wrote about a "holy dissatisfaction" with things as they are. Is this good or bad?

92. Not Status—But Stature
Philippians 4:1-11

1. Vance Packard relates in his book *The Status Seekers* the thought that there are at least five classes of people in our society: (1) The Real Upper Class, (2) the Semi-upper Class, (3) The Limited Success Group, (4) The Working Class, (5) The Real Lower Class.

2. Do you think there are classes in our society such as they used to have in Europe?

3. What are some of the dangers of class distinction?

4. How should we measure our success?

5. In many colleges and universities there are sororities and fraternities which you can enter only if you have been chosen. Can you see any dangers inherent in such organizations? Is it not better that people of the same financial class live together?

6. There is undoubtedly a distinction in the social level of churches. It seems natural that people of the same social class join together, for example, a "down town" church or one in the suburbs. Is this good or bad? Is it inevitable?

7. What are some of the status symbols among us? Among our young people?

8. Do you think it would be wise for a girl of relatively poor parents to marry a young man from a millionaire family? What would be some of the problems?

9. Paul tells us to be "content." Does this mean that we have to be satisfied with whatever we have, or may we also strive to improve ourselves?

10. Why is there so little real contentment today?

11. How can we show our Christian "stature" in distinction from "status"?

12. Can a person be too content? Should we not develop a bit of "holy dissatisfaction"?

93. Respect for Authority
Colossians 3:18-25

1. Is it true that all authority is from God? Is there such a thing as God-given authority?

2. The basic form of authority is in the home. Is it possible for parents to be too authoritarian in dealing with their children? Should children always obey the commands of their parents?

3. Should we respect a person such as a minister, doctor or elder for the sake of the position they have, or only when they are worthy of our respect?

4. When is it right to disobey those in authority over us, such as a foreman in a factory, a doctor or nurse in a hospital, or the government of a country?

5. If we think that the orders given by a superior are wrong, how should we handle the situation?

6. Children should obey their parents. At what age do you think a child need no longer obey his parents, but can begin to think for himself?

7. If children do not respect their parents, is this the fault of the parents or of the children?

8. Who are the authorities in your church? Do we obey them because of their position, or only when we think they are in the right?

9. Do older people have a right to expect that younger people respect them because of their age, or only when they are worthy of our respect?

10. If you work in a factory and think that the foreman has it in for you and picks on you, what is the Christian thing to do?

11. Would you join in a protest march for causes such as civil rights and stop-the-war?

12. If you are a person who has authority over others, what responsibilities does this give you?

94. Toward Greater Maturity
II Timothy 3:14-17

1. No one in this life is fully mature, but we must have this as our goal. What is wrong with immaturity in an adult?

2. A mature person finds joy in giving as well as in receiving. Why do parents need a great deal of this quality? How can we develop this in ourselves?

3. A mature person can form permanent loyalties. Is there anything you can do about it if you do not have this ability?

4. A mature person can make decisions and carry them out. Why do some people find it so hard to make choices? When should children begin to make choices in life?

5. A mature person can make decisions gracefully. What experiences help us to be able to rise above the competition of our present age?

6. A mature person lives above the level of hostility and aggressiveness. Why are there so many hostilities among people today? How can we overcome these?

7. A mature person has learned to be flexible and adaptable. Some people find it hard to change their minds or their feelings toward others. How does such a rigid spirit develop? How can it be overcome?

8. A mature person develops a seasoned faith. What is wrong with a young person who uses religious language that we would normally expect of an older person? How does our faith help us to become more mature?

9. A mature person has a healthy view of death. What must be our attitude toward death? Some people are overly fearful about their heart or the fact that they might have cancer. Why?

10. Do you think that our present form of government helps to make people more mature or less mature?

95. Adorning the Gospel
Titus 2:1-10

1. Paul is speaking here to slaves. Does the Bible condemn slavery? Does it condone it?

2. How can we adorn the gospel? Is it not already as attractive and beautiful as it can be?

3. We test the teachings and the isms of men by the lives of those who profess to believe in them. We ask, "How does it work out in the lives of those who are members of a given religion?" Is this a fair way to judge such isms as Communism or Mohammedanism?

4. The gospel makes some tremendous claims. It will transform our hearts and lives, it takes away our sins, it will help us to overcome worry and give peace of heart. Does it seem as though the gospel really does that in the lives of people today?

5. It has been reported that missionaries often found that their work was hampered by traders and tourists. What does this show about the lives of these people?

6. Often people have refused to join the church because there are so many hypocrites and inconsistent Christians in the church. Is this a good excuse? What should the Church do about this condition?

7. Paul tells the slaves to adorn the gospel in all things. What are the things they must do to adorn the gospel? Are they big things or little ones? Verses 9 and 10.

8. How should we adorn the gospel today?

9. Someone has said, "If we would adorn the gospel of Christ we must first allow the gospel to adorn us." How is this accomplished?

10. What does it mean to try to live above the average?

96. Should We Let Our Conscience Be Our Guide?

Psalm 119:9-16; Hebrews 9:11-14

1. Someone writes that to say, "Let your conscience be your guide" is a denial of the principle that the Bible is our only guide for faith and conduct. What do you think of this statement?

2. Some people have a very sensitive conscience. Does this mean that they are better Christians, or are they only more narrow-minded?

3. How much does our training in the home influence our conscience? If our parents are strict, will this also make our conscience more sensitive?

4. One person may say, "It doesn't bother my conscience to go to a professional ball game on Sunday." Another will say, "It does bother mine." How can you tell which of these two is correct?

5. In some countries it is considered to be a good thing to allow mentally retarded children to die by exposure. Their conscience tells them this is the thing to do. Does this show that conscience is not reliable?

6. A business man sold his business and decided to go to the mission field. When asked why he did this he said, "I have to live with my conscience." What does this mean? Is it good to use conscience as a guide at such a time?

7. Do you think our emotions influence our response to conscience? Is a person who is quite emotional also more responsive to his conscience?

8. Why are some people overly conscientious? What is wrong with this?

9. How must we handle a guilty conscience?

10. Is there such a thing as a regenerated conscience?

11. Was there a conscience in paradise? Will man have a conscience in heaven?

97. Moses—The Secret of Endurance
Hebrews 11:23-31

1. The Bible often mentions "endurance." This implies the ability to persevere, to withstand frustration and temptation, to carry on in spite of difficulties. Why is this so important?

2. Does a lack of endurance show a weakness of character? Examples would be college drop-outs, marriages that begin well but soon deteriorate, society meetings in the church.

3. Moses endured the temptation of prosperity in Pharaoh's palace. Why do many people find it hard to persevere in days of prosperity? Do you think people are spoiled by affluence today? Do you think "the great society" is good for people?

4. Moses withstood the test of solitude. Why do many people find it hard to be alone?

5. Moses persevered in the routine of daily work. Why do people view their daily work as drudgery? Is this due to the nature of the work or the attitude they take toward it?

6. Moses withstood the frustrations that were a part of leadership in the nation of Israel. Many people today are easily upset by frustrating things. Why? What can we do about it?

7. The secret of endurance is described as "seeing him who is invisible." How can a person see the "invisible One"?

8. In what way does the vision of God affect us in our daily life? In the face of life's temptations?

9. Do you feel that endurance is only a spiritual quality, or is it a trait of character? Is it something we develop in childhood?

10. There are people who never seem to finish the things they do or the things they make. How can they overcome this?

98. Inconsistencies
James 1:1-11

1. There is a lot of inconsistency in all our lives.

–A staunch member of the church may drive a hard bargain in his business.

–Some people are very pleasant and congenial when others are around, but hard to live with in their own family.

2. What is wrong with people who are extremely inconsistent?

3. We often use the term "compartmentalization." This is one of the defense reactions we use in solving our conflicts. How does this affect a person in his religious life? In his work? In his home life?

4. Does our doctrine and our life ever fully agree? Do we ever completely practice what we preach? Is this consistency?

5. In what way is the man who worries too much inconsistent?

6. How can we develop greater consistency in our lives? Is this a matter of our Christian faith, or our character and personality, or both?

7. James describes the inconsistent man as "unstable in all his ways." What does he mean?

8. How does inconsistency reveal itself in the following:

   –in the race question?
   –in our entertainment?
   –in status seeking?

9. Do you think there is such a person as a consistent Christian?

99. Learning to Make Decisions
James 1:1-11

1. God gave man the power of choice, this is a function of the human mind and life. Why do some people find it so hard to make choices?

2. What effect will our earlier training have on our ability to make decisions?

3. Does indecision show a lack of self-confidence, or is it just a bad habit that we get into?

4. If you have a hard time deciding which dress or shirt to buy, is it better to have someone else go with you to help you, or should you make up your own mind?

5. Someone said, "I've made up my mind; don't come with any more arguments, for it will only confuse me." Is this a good attitude?

6. Some people make up their minds and then refuse to change, even though others think they are wrong. Is this good, or are they just stubborn?

7. In making decisions we need some standard of judgment. What standard should we use when choosing our life's work? Our life's mate? Our church?

8. When we make a decision that is contrary to what most other people choose, does this mean that we are wrong? How can we tell?

9. Should we choose with our head, with our heart, or with both?

10. Umpires in big league baseball games often have to make difficult decisions. Usually, when they have made a decision they do not change it no matter how much protest they receive. What kind of men are they?

100. Facing Temptations
I Corinthians 10:12, 13; James 1:12-18

1. We are all subject to temptations. Are we tempted by Satan or does the temptation come from our own sinful nature?

2. Do you think some people suffer greater temptations than others? Is this because of their work, or do they needlessly place themselves in the way of temptation?

3. Some people seem to fall into temptation more than others. Why is this so?

4. What does Jesus mean when He teaches us to pray, "Lead us not into temptation?" Do we pray to be kept from temptation, or to be kept in temptation?

5. Give some practical ways of overcoming temptation.

6. Do you think a lazy man is just giving in to temptation, or is this a habit? How about a person who curses? Or one who is impatient?

7. Is an alcoholic a person who is weak in the face of temptation, or is he sick?

8. Do you think God's people suffer more temptations than unbelievers? Why?

9. Does God ever tempt us? Does He allow us to be tempted? Why would a loving God allow His people to be tempted?

10. What does the promise in I Corinthians 10:13 mean to you?

11. Do we ever sin without being tempted?

12. Jesus was sinless, and yet He was tempted to sin. How is this possible? Was this a real temptation?

13. There was a temptation in the Garden of Eden. How can there be temptation in such surroundings?

14. What are some of the temptations that come to us in church? While we are at prayer?

101. Learning to Be Patient
Hebrews 12:1-6; James 5:7-11

1. The Greek word used for *patience* suggests two ideas: forbearance and endurance. It means a willingness to wait, and persistence to achieve a goal.

2. Do you think we are born patient, or is this something we must learn? Is it correct to say that an impatient person is also immature?

3. What are some of the things that test our patience?

4. Some people are able to suffer patiently when they are sick, but they get very impatient when they have to wait fifteen minutes for their mate. How do you explain this?

5. Can a person be too patient? Is it good that a sick person just waits patiently, or should he be a bit impatient to get well again?

6. It takes patience to learn a new skill or a new language. What kind of patience is this?

7. What kind of patience does Job show in his life?

8. How does our faith help us to be more patient in times of illness?

9. Is it true that the person who becomes panicky is usually an impatient person?

10. How can we learn to become more patient?

102. Controlling Our Tongues
James 3:1-12

1. There is great power in words, such as: words of comfort, counsel, or advice; or words of anger, untruth, gossip, or enticing others to sin.

2. Why are words so important to us? Someone said that he would rather be blind than deaf. How do you feel about this?

3. Why are some people more talkative than others? When a person does not talk much, what does this show us about the person?

4. Are there little white lites? Social lies? Justifiable lies?

5. Should a person always tell the whole truth?

6. When does telling something about others become gossip?

7. What are some of the dangers and results of slander? Do you think a Christian should ever sue another person for slander?

8. Modern biographies often stress that they tell the unvarnished truth about a person. Is it good to do this, such as in the book, *The Hidden Lincoln*?

9. Why do people feel the need of using profanity?

10. Some people tell "smutty stories." What does this tell us about such a person? Why are many of the best-sellers in books the ones that emphasize sex? Is it good for us to read these books? Should we expose our children to these books?

11. In what way should we make use of our speech in a positive and constructive way? How can we glorify God by our speech?

103. Faith and Healing
Mark 2:1-12

1. Jesus' ministry was one of healing as well as of teaching. What was the purpose of His healing ministry? Mark 2:9-11.

2. The disciples and also Paul had the power to heal. Was there a special purpose for this in the early church? Does this still hold for today?

3. Why did not Paul heal himself from the "thorn in the flesh"? Why didn't he heal Epaphroditus (Phil. 2:26).

4. Jesus often said, "Thy faith hath made thee whole." Was faith necessary for the healing miracles of Christ?

5. The passage in James is often quoted as a proof that there is still the power of healing in the church. Do you think that this passage applies to the kind of healing of Oral Roberts and others?

6. Many people go to such shrines as the one in Lourdes, France. It is claimed that 10 percent of those who go there are helped. How do you explain the help that is received there? Is this faith healing?

7. What is God's purpose in sending sickness and suffering?

8. Faith healers say, "God does not will sickness." How do you feel about this? If God does not send our illnesses, who does?

9. How would you feel about having healing services in your church?

10. What is your reaction to the statement, "I believe in faith healing, but I do not believe in faith healers"?

11. Does our faith have anything to do with our sicknesses, either of the body or of the mind? If there were more faith among men, would there be less illness?

12. How does faith help us to accept our illnesses?